ABOVE

AND

BEYOND

THE ILLUSTRATED STORY OF
MISSION AVIATION FELLOWSHIP

In memory of Stuart King
1922 – 2020

Now to him who is able to do above and beyond all that
we ask or think according to the power that works in us —
to him be glory in the church and in Christ Jesus to all
generations, forever and ever. Amen.

Ephesians 3:20-21 (CSB)

First published in Great Britain in 2020 by
Mission Aviation Fellowship UK
Castle Hill Avenue, Folkestone, Kent CT20 2TN
Email: supporter.relations@maf-uk.org
Website: www.maf.uk.org

Mission Aviation Fellowship UK is part of Mission Aviation
Fellowship International.

A CIP catalogue record for this book is available
from the British Library.

ISBN 978-0-992-71603-5 Hardback
[ISBN 978-0-992-71604-2 Limited paperback]

Designed and typeset by MAF UK

Printed and bound in the United Kingdom by Bell & Bain Ltd

Foreword

Touching the lives of those who are hard-to-reach runs through the life and work of Jesus and is at the very heart of the Church's work worldwide.

It has been an honour and privilege to be part of the Christian mission, travelling across the globe to speak the peace and hope of Christ to those who are suffering. During my time as Archbishop, I have travelled to many parts of the world to communities that are living in situations of conflict and need.

Mission Aviation Fellowship is an inspiring and exceptional organisation at the very heart of God's rescue plan for our broken world. Having flown numerous times on board MAF's trusted and unique aircraft, I have witnessed first-hand how God is using this remarkable charity to bring life and hope to some of the most hard-to-reach people on earth. I remember particularly travelling on an MAF aircraft to Bor in South Sudan in 2014, to a city that had been devastated by civil war. MAF provided that lifeline to a community separated and marginalised by a terrible conflict.

Above and Beyond offers a beautiful and inspiring account of how the Kingdom of God has spread to those who are in great need, through the faith, vision, and obedience of MAF throughout many exciting decades.

I am pleased to have been part of this life-changing story.

+ Tust Cantuar:

The Most Reverend and Right Honourable Justin Welby, Archbishop of Canterbury

Imagine a place where there are no roads.

Cut off from the outside world.

Isolated.

Imagine a place hemmed in by mountains...

Where trees are as thick and dense as walls...

... or all you can see is sand.

A place surrounded by water...

... a place many days trek by land.

What if there was a plane?

***Mission Aviation Fellowship is the world's
largest humanitarian airline.***

Overcoming natural barriers using aviation and
technology, MAF has been serving isolated communities
since 1945.

This book shares the fascinating MAF story and unpacks
the early vision, lifesaving impact and ongoing challenges
behind this worldwide mission.

Today, an MAF aircraft takes off or lands every five
minutes around the developing world.

ISOLATED PEOPLE

MAF's earliest vision was to support missions who were serving people in places that were difficult or impossible to reach by other means. Communities that were isolated by difficult terrain, the lack of roads, adverse weather conditions, or where overland travel was too dangerous because of war, conflict or bandits.

MAF knows by experience that isolated communities face additional hardships due to the difficulty of accessing healthcare, education and other services that many may take for granted.

In 2015, all United Nations member states adopted the 2030 Agenda for Sustainable Development to create strategies to tackle the most intractable causes of poverty and inequality around the world. The 17 Sustainable Development Goals (SDGs) were established. These goals provide a framework from which plans to reduce extreme poverty, improve access to healthcare and other factors vital to human flourishing, may be developed and monitored.

The SDGs reflect MAF's belief that every community, however remote, should have the essentials for life, but the UN has highlighted that geographical distance and insecure or dangerous travel are barriers to the achievement of the SDGs.

Therefore the UN has stated, 'We pledge that no one will be left behind, and we will endeavour to reach the furthest behind first.'

So – in an echo of Matthew 19:30 – 'many who are last will be first.'

Organisations around the world are working tirelessly to improve the lives of the poorest and most vulnerable communities but they know that the highest rates of disability, malaria, maternal mortality – and those most lacking in healthcare, education and equality – are frequently in the most remote areas.

A major problem for many NGOs and missions is the lack of safe, reliable travel but MAF's flights provide the perfect solution. By flying partner organisations to isolated communities, MAF helps to overcome these barriers.

MAF has always applied the principle of 'leave no one behind' to both physical and spiritual poverty, which has enabled the work of mission organisations, Bible translators and distributors, and local churches across the world reach those most in need.

Betty Greene helps form
Christian Airmen's Missionary
Fellowship (CAMF) in the **USA**

End of WWII, Stuart King joins
early pioneers to open **Mission**
Aviation Fellowship's (MAF)
London office

CAMF buys its first aircraft,
1933 Waco Cabin biplane

Betty Greene becomes first female
MAF pilot to fly across the **Andes**
in Grumman Duck aircraft

CAMF changes its name to **MAF**

First mission surveys in **Mexico, Ecuador**
and **Peru**, piloted by Betty Greene

1944   **1945**   **1946**   **1946/1947**

1

EARLY INSPIRATION

As fighting raged across Europe, Christian airmen and airwomen from Britain, the USA and Australia began to dream of peace. Peace that would bring hope, stability and a chance for aircraft to be used for good rather than for war.

Using their wartime experience, skills, and strong Christian faith, a handful of inspirational pioneers crafted a movement that would shape the future of mission aviation and pave a way for aircraft to reach the most isolated corners of the globe with the love of God.

Missionary Aviation Fellowship founded in Melbourne, **Australia**

MAF launches an operation in Chiapas state, **Mexico**

MAF acquires its first Miles Gemini aircraft in the **UK**

Nate Saint establishes regular flight service for missionaries in **Ecuador** under the name Alas de Socorro

MAF's first survey flight from **London to Africa** by Stuart King and Jack Hemmings

Murray Kendon returns to **New Zealand** to launch MAF in **Asia Pacific**

MAF buys a de Havilland Rapide aircraft for **Sudan**

1947   **1948**   **1949**   **1949**

BETTY GREENE

In February 1946, Elizabeth Everts 'Betty' Greene made history as the pilot of the first ever MAF flight. A pioneering woman of faith, passion and great talent, she spearheaded the mission aviation movement in the USA.

Below, left:
Betty Greene with Waco Standard Cabin biplane, Southern Mexico

Below, right:
Aerial view of Andes Mountains

Opposite, top to bottom: *Betty in service with WASPs*

Betty Greene repairing cloth plane in Sudan, circa 1950

Betty Greene seated in the cockpit of the Waco, ready to depart for Mexico

Betty had developed an early love of aviation. Longing for travel and adventure, she took flying lessons as a teenager, culminating in a solo flight.

After serving with the Women Airforce Service Pilots (WASPs) in World War II, she was only 25 years old when she took to the skies again, achieving another first as a female mission pilot:

'On the morning of our departure, a group of friends gathered for prayer and to wish us well. After taxiing to the east end of the dirt strip, I swung the plane around for take-off.' The very first MAF flight was underway.

The excitement was tangible on that first flight from Los Angeles, California in the beautiful red 1933 four-seater Waco Standard Cabin biplane. Its two passengers were from Wycliffe Bible Translators, joining others for training at 'Jungle Camp' south of Mexico City. Staff of Wycliffe Bible Translators spread out across Asia, Africa and Latin America to translate the Bible into scores of indigenous languages.

'What a thrill to actually be doing the work for which we had hoped, prayed and planned,'

Betty wrote in her book *Flying High*.

The journey took more than three days as Betty proceeded cautiously, grounding the plane at one point to investigate a concern with the engine which, fortunately, turned out to be nothing more than flaking paint. These early flights were a steep learning curve for the young pilot – building on her wartime experience flying several kinds of military planes, towing aerial targets for artillery practice and participating in experimental stratospheric flight testing.

One lesson learned early on was the need for wide safety margins when flying over mountainous areas. Betty

Los Angeles

UNITED STATES OF AMERICA

MEXICO

Mexico City

GUATEMALA

'encountered an unusually severe downdraft' crossing mountains near Arriaga:

'A glance at the rate of climb indicator told me that we were descending at about 2,000 feet per minute, although I was in level flight and had level throttle. Fortunately, I had several thousand feet to spare and was glad of it.' Disaster was avoided and valuable knowledge gained.

An understanding of the challenges involved in flying in tropical climates and over remote and difficult terrain had to be learned on the job by Betty and the other early pioneers. This was later passed on to generations of MAF bush pilots through excellent training.

Betty went on to serve in 12 countries including Peru, Nigeria, Sudan and Papua, Indonesia and touched down in some 20 more, before returning in 1962 to serve MAF from its American base. Her impact as a woman and a pilot was clear. 'I was frequently the first woman pilot to fly in an area,' she explained.

'It was said that I was the first to fly across the Peruvian Andes into the jungles of the upper reaches of the Amazon River. In Sudan, it took an act of parliament for me to fly there. In Papua, no woman had piloted a plane into the so-recently opened interior.

'These experiences were thrilling but, in all honesty, I did not have any ambition to achieve 'firsts' in flying. My mind was set on doing productive work and any achievements in flying came about incidentally, as I carried out my assignments.'

Betty's resilience and grace when continually facing resistance as a female pilot in a man's world, were remarkable. She was decades ahead of her time and God's chosen instrument for an important strategic role in MAF's early development. ✠

THE FLEET:
WACO UIC STANDARD CABIN

The honour of the first MAF flight belongs to Betty Greene and the bright-red Waco Standard Cabin biplane in which she took off from La Habra, California, USA on 23 February 1946.

Betty Greene was bound for Mexico to set up the first flight programme for what was then called Christian Airmen's Missionary Fellowship (CAMF), supporting the mission of Wycliffe Bible Translators.

Much thought had gone into selecting an appropriate aircraft for this work. Initially, a light aircraft such as a Piper Family Cruiser was the preferred option; however, the kind of flying that would be undertaken in Mexico, which included moving bulky and heavy supplies over considerable distances, meant that a larger aircraft would be more suitable. Eventually the

> **❝**
>
> **The brand-new 220hp Continental R-670 radial engine afforded it enough power to easily reach 13,000ft and its serviceability and reliability were superb.**

CAMF team identified the pre-war Waco biplanes as their best option and in February 1946 a newly-rebuilt 1933 Waco UIC Standard Cabin was purchased for what was regarded as a bargain price of $5,000.

Once in Mexico, the four-seater aircraft immediately proved itself to be an excellent performer; the brand-new 220hp Continental R-670 radial engine afforded it enough power to easily reach 13,000ft and its serviceability and reliability

Right: Early CAMF team

Opposite: Betty Greene in front of plane

GENERAL CHARACTERISTICS

Crew
one

Capacity
three passengers

Length
7.67m (25ft 2in)

Overall Wingspan
10.13m (33ft 3in)

Height
2.6m (8ft 6in)

Empty weight
767kg (1,690lb)

Gross weight
1,270kg (2,800lb)

Powerplant
one Continental R-670,
220hp (164kW)

Propeller
two-blade fixed-pitch

PERFORMANCE

Max. speed
121kn (224km/h, 140mph)

Cruise speed
102kn (190km/h, 118mph)

Stall speed
42kn (79km/h, 49mph)

Range
478nmi (885km, 550mi)

Service ceiling
14,000ft

were superb. The Waco's biplane configuration was something of a mixed blessing when operating from unprepared jungle airstrips; while it gave the aircraft good short-field performance, the lower wings restricted downward visibility and were prone to damage. Almost all subsequent MAF aircraft have been high-wing monoplanes partly for this reason.

Sadly, however, the Waco's active service was to be very short-lived. On 26 March 1946, little over a month after leaving the USA, the aircraft was being flown by a newly-arrived CAMF pilot, George Wiggins. Deep in the jungle at El Real, Mexico, Wiggins collided with a hut at the edge of the airstrip while landing, seriously damaging the port wings, propeller and

landing gear. Wiggins and Greene both emerged from the aircraft completely unharmed, but the Waco itself was in a terrible state.

Without any personnel in-country qualified to undertake the major structural repairs required, the CAMF leadership asked Nate Saint to travel overland to Mexico. The repairs would take until December to complete and are an extraordinary tale of resolve and ingenuity. The Waco was safely flown out of the El Real airstrip by Wiggins, but once back in Mexico City the decision was taken to sell the aircraft. Unable to locate any buyers in Mexico, the Waco was eventually flown back to California, where it was sold for $500. ✚

MURRAY KENDON

New Zealander Murray Kendon was the visionary behind the formation of MAF in the UK and its early work in Africa. Revealing the inspiration behind the vision, Murray shares part of his story:

Main: Jack Hemmings, Murray Kendon, Stuart King & Ken Ellis preparing the Gemini 'Mildmay Pathfinder' before their first survey flight

Opposite, top to bottom: Murray Kendon; the Pathfinder team in the Gemini including Tom Banham (far right); Murray Kendon's letter to the Mildmay Outlook, March 1945

'I was converted in 1933, at the age of 16. From then on, I was working to bring others to the Lord.

With time, an urgency grew in Murray's heart. 'I wanted to find a way to get the message of the reality of true life in Jesus Christ to those living far away from a city or town, especially to the young people.'

Having sought God's guidance with a like-minded Christian friend, 'We left our work and homes in early 1937 to sing and preach in small townships and scattered settlements.' They held evangelistic meetings throughout New Zealand into the early years of World War II, when they were no longer allowed to buy petrol for such work. Murray was called up for military service in 1942 and entered the air force.

As a Flight Lieutenant in 179 squadron, Murray flew Wellington bombers. 'Our brief was to find and destroy the enemy submarines combing the Atlantic to sink allied ships carrying troops, fuel or supplies to Britain.

> ## How is it that there is enough money to get thousands of planes into the air to kill and destroy, when only a handful are being used for missionary work?

'One night, while flying over the Bay of Biscay on U-boat patrol, I could see in the distance the flak coming from the antiaircraft guns as the searchlights were scanning the sky over France, looking for a British 'thousand bomber raid'.

'I remembered hearing years before about a team that had set out to find a tribe, said to be living somewhere deep in the jungle. The missionaries returned weeks later, out of food and worn out by the incredible hardship, having almost been killed by a flash flood that destroyed their canoe. I thought, 'a small aeroplane could have found that tribe and mapped a route all in a day or two, and later guided the team, dropping supplies to them.'

In 1945 Murray wrote to The Movement for World Evangelization, more commonly known as the Mildmay Movement. Together they explored the idea of a Christian air service to support missionaries. Through their small publication, the *Mildmay Outlook*, they invited responses from interested Christian airmen to be in contact. Having registered MAF as an

organisation in 1945, Murray shared more about their plans in a subsequent issue:

'At last! After six, dragging, difficult years of war, we have a breathing space in which to return with new vigour and hope to the holy task of spreading the Good News of salvation to the farthest corners of the earth.

'Many inventions of modern days lend themselves readily to the furtherance of the Gospel, chief among them being the radio and the aeroplane. The radio can speed its message around the world in less than a seventh of a second. The aeroplane can do more than speed the message of salvation, it can hasten the transport of man with the message. Let us cut down, in the missionary's life, the terrific amount of time and money wasted in slow and tedious methods of transport.

'Aircraft have been used in large numbers to carry sudden destruction to the cities of our enemies…Realising the tremendous issues at stake, we were ready to give to the point of sacrifice, money, time, energy, life itself, even our loved ones, to make it possible for this new weapon to prove itself in battle.

— **"** —

Why should not aircraft be even more effectively used to carry messengers of peace and to unload cargoes of blessing? Instead of spreading destruction and death why should they not now spread life and healing by that message wherein lie the seeds of peace and power?

'Christian men and women, let us now make that sacrifice for Christ which we were willing to make for our country. Let us enable the aeroplane to prove its worth in the spiritual battle.

'There is much more to missionary aviation than buying a number of aircraft and sending them out with their pilots. Landing strips and hangars must be built, equipment installed, and supplies of petrol, oil and spares arranged. The aircraft must be properly maintained by qualified engineers, and flown to a schedule designed for overall economy.

'An air transport service is needed, organised separately and undertaking all details, but working for and in co-operation with all evangelical missionaries in a given sphere.'

Through the *Mildmay Outlook*, Murray reached the likes of RAF engineer Stuart King, squadron leader Jack Hemmings and others who responded to the invitation to the calling. ✚

THE MILDMAY MOVEMENT

The Movement for World Evangelization, more commonly known as the Mildmay Movement, was established by Dr Thomas Cochrane with three primary areas of focus: evangelism, prayer and world survey. Its surveys demonstrated the immensity of the job confronting the Christian Church:

"The task of world evangelism is so vast that we must make the best use of all resources that are available and evangelistic effort must be undertaken in those areas where survey reveals outstanding need or opportunities of strategic importance."

The Mildmay Outlook, **March 1945**

STUART KING

Born in London in 1922, Stuart Sendall-King was interested in aviation from an early age. Tasting RAF life as a member of the Cardiff University Air Squadron, he completed an engineering degree and had high hopes of becoming a pilot.

It was 1941 and engineers were in high demand to power Britain through WWII. 'We don't want you as a pilot,' said the Wing Commander crisply at Stuart's selection interview. 'We can train a pilot in six months in wartime – it takes us three years to train an engineer officer.' Stuart's career had been taken out of his hands.

As the engineer officer for 247 Fighter Squadron during the early invasion of France, Stuart found himself caught in the deafening, life-changing chaos of war.

Receiving an article from his mother written by Murray Kendon, Stuart was intrigued by the early visions of MAF. He wrote to Murray with ideas and technical advice, only to receive a clear reply: Murray was less interested in Stuart's ideas and more interested in him.

Returning to Duxford in 1945 to map out his permanent commission in the RAF, Stuart's official invitation to join MAF was the least attractive option on the table. But God had other plans.

> ## ❝
> **Stuart and Jack prepared for their six-month mission to explore the basic question of whether aircraft could assist with the work of humanitarian missionaries dotted across Africa.**

Squadron Leader Jack Hemmings joined Stuart when he stumbled almost by accident into the Mildmay operations room after being demobilised from the RAF in New Zealand as God eloquently added to MAF's numbers, vision and skills.

Funds were rallied for MAF's first aircraft – a Miles Gemini – from a handful of pilots and friends in 1947. Stuart and Jack prepared for their six-month mission to explore the basic question of whether aircraft could assist the work of humanitarian missionaries dotted across Africa. With little more than a map, compass and their wartime RAF experience, the

Main: Jack Hemmings & Stuart King during the 1948 survey flight to Africa

Opposite page, clockwise from top-right: the Mildmay Outlook, March 1945; Stuart & Phyllis with John & Rebecca, 1957; cartoon by Stuart King; Stuart King in his RAF uniform

"Together with my flight sergeant, I threw myself to the ground. A Focke-Wulf cannon shell splintered through the timbers two feet above my head. Around us, the whole airfield was in chaos: smoke rising, planes full of holes, transport vehicles ablaze. The smell of burning oil filled the air. As soon as the attacking planes disappeared, we rushed to get the injured to hospital. A few of our maintenance staff were among them, some already dying.

Five months later, the war in Europe ended. I was allowed a couple of weeks' home leave and spent part of it at a young people's holiday conference. On the final evening, the leader asked, 'Will those who want God really to take and control their lives, please stand.' I knew I couldn't live a halfway-Christian life any longer. That moment was a turning point in my life.

Like many others, I wanted to see lasting peace. But even more than that, I wanted to see people find the peace of God in their hearts. What could be more exciting than sharing it?"

Extract from *Hope Has Wings*, Stuart King, 2004, pp32-33

fearless pair plotted a route across Libya, Egypt, Sudan, Kenya and the Belgian Congo (now the Democratic Republic of the Condo, or DRC) and took off from Croydon Airport, UK on 13 January 1948, using the River Nile as their guide.

Discovering hazardous terrain and unimaginable needs, Stuart and Jack established connections with the missionary community and ascertained that in many places, the only way to bring about life-transforming help in the wilderness was to build airstrips. It was an adventure of a lifetime and one they both embraced with fearless determination and a healthy dose of pragmatic humour.

Meeting his wife Phyllis, a missionary working in Sudan, in 1951 Stuart began a romance, marriage and life-long partnership with a woman who

embraced his determination to share God's love through aviation. The pair journeyed across Africa with their three children, Rebecca, John and Cilla and saw their early hopes for a humanitarian air service expand across Sudan, Africa and the world.

For over 70 years, Stuart was at the heart of an organisation which grew and expanded beyond his expectation. Since that initial hair-raising survey in 1948, MAF has held to Stuart, Jack and Murray's founding vision of using aviation to reach isolated people with practical care and spiritual hope.

Stuart committed to raising his own finances and survived on basic missionary funding from 1945 to 1985, when he handed over to a new Chief Executive and took a six-month sabbatical. Contributing to MAF UK Board meetings and becoming President Emeritus of MAF International in 1987, Stuart's dedication and commitment to MAF never ceased. Retiring in Folkestone, close to the MAF UK headquarters, Stuart regularly visited the offices and never failed to inspire the growing team who were taking MAF into the next chapter of its history. ✠

"It had been my habit to take time every morning before breakfast to read a passage from the Bible. I had been going through Hebrews, one morning reading chapter 11: *'By faith Abraham... went out... not knowing where he was going.'* (Hebrews 11:8 ESV)

In a flash, I knew that verse was for me. My future was not to be with the known RAF, or with the established aircraft industry. I had to step out in faith and join MAF."

Extract from *Hope Has Wings*, Stuart King, 2004, p35

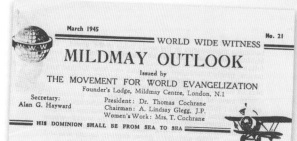

March 1945 — WORLD WIDE WITNESS — No. 21

MILDMAY OUTLOOK

Issued by
THE MOVEMENT FOR WORLD EVANGELIZATION
Founder's Lodge, Mildmay Centre, London, N.1

Secretary:
Alan G. Hayward

President: Dr. Thomas Cochrane
Chairman: A. Lindsay Glegg, J.P.
Women's Work: Mrs. T. Cochrane

HIS DOMINION SHALL BE FROM SEA TO SEA

THE NEXT STEP.

It is well from time to time both for our own sakes and for the sake of our readers to remind ourselves of the basis upon which our work is built and of the Mildmay outlook, so that we will briefly go back to the beginnings of our work and look again at the goal.

In 1911, Dr. Cochrane surveyed the Christian situation throughout China, where he was then Founder and Principal of the Union Medical College, and succeeded in getting a group together to finance and supply the most exhaustive missionary survey ever made. Whilst this survey confined itself to China the interest it created led to the conception of world survey and ultimately to the creation of the World Dominion Movement. This Movement stood, and still stands, for three things.

(1) Continuous world survey. (2) Indigenous principles. (3) World evangelization.

It is not an exaggeration to say that this Movement has affected Christian thinking on every mission field of the world. Its surveys succeeded in demonstrating the immensity of the task confronting the Christian Church. It was in order that the facts so revealed might be effective to the ultimate aim of world evangelization that the Mildmay Movement was formed.

The Mildmay Movement not only creates interest in the three aims of the World Dominion Movement, but sets in motion evangelistic campaigns at home and overseas—campaigns which strike a distinctive missionary note and result in the addition of forces and resources to promote world evangelization.

"SOMETIMES WE DIDN'T QUITE KNOW JUST WHERE WE WERE"

THE FLEET:
MILES GEMINI

'Altogether, a beautiful little aircraft...'

In the immediate aftermath of World War II, huge numbers of pre-war and war-surplus aircraft were available for purchase. With so much choice on offer, selecting a suitable aircraft for MAF's initial survey of East Africa was a surprisingly complex process. The chosen plane would have to be reliable and rugged, with simple systems that could be easily serviced in isolated locations with limited resources. As the survey flights would use improvised airstrips, the aircraft would also have to be small enough to land in restrictive spaces and be blessed with good 'short field' performance.

> ❝
> **This robustness would soon be put to the test when Jack made a forced landing in a rutted field...**

After extensive discussion, testing and evaluation of all available options, the Miles M.65 Gemini was eventually chosen for this historic journey. However, this was neither a pre-war, nor war-surplus aircraft. The Gemini design was in fact a brand-new one, having first flown in October 1945. It was sleek and modern, later described by Stuart King as 'altogether a beautiful little aircraft' and perhaps looked more suited to life as an executive plaything than as a tool for missionary work!

Advertised by the British company Miles Aircraft as 'the safest light aeroplane in the world', the aircraft purchased by MAF was a Gemini 1A, the standard production variant, fitted with twin Blackburn Cirrus Minor II engines. These compact power units developed a combined total of 200hp, with each driving a two-bladed, fixed-pitch propeller, allowing the Gemini to cruise at a respectable 120mph when fully laden. The twin-engined design gave the Gemini an extra safety margin over a single-engined aircraft in the event of engine failure, which was a serious consideration given the long distances that the crew would be flying over extremely inhospitable terrain.

As a post-war design, the Gemini boasted modern features such as an electrically-operated retractable undercarriage which reduced drag and improved performance once airborne and large, powerful flaps allowing slower, shorter landings. Constructed of spruce and plywood, which was then covered with madapolin, a fine, lightweight cloth, the Gemini was a relatively rugged aeroplane. This robustness would soon be put to the test when Jack Hemmings made a forced landing in a rutted field after a failed take-off from Asmara, Ethiopia.

However, the 1948 survey flights revealed some of the Gemini's limitations. In particular, the radio equipment lacked sufficient range and

> ❝
> **Caught in powerful downdrafts in Burundi, they amazingly escaped without serious injury.**

the normally-aspirated Cirrus Minor engines struggled in the hot, thin air found in some of the locations where MAF planned to operate. These and other performance deficiencies were to provide critical learning points for future MAF operations.

Ultimately, the Gemini's operational service with the fledgling MAF was a very brief one. Caught in powerful downdrafts in the mountains of Burundi, Jack Hemmings and Stuart King were unable to avoid impacting the ground and destroying the aircraft, although they amazingly escaped without serious injury.

This crash again highlighted the performance deficiencies of the Gemini, which was simply underpowered for the kind of flying that MAF would demand. However, despite its shortcomings and ignominious end, Miles M.65 Gemini A1 G-AJZK played a crucial and valuable role in the MAF story. ✈

FACTFILE

GENERAL CHARACTERISTICS

Crew
one

Capacity
three passengers

Length
6.78m (22ft 3in)

Wingspan
11.02m (36ft 2in)

Height
2.29m (7ft 6in)

Wing area
17.7m² (191sq. ft)

Empty weight
866kg (1,910lb)

Max. take off weight
1,361kg (3,000lb)

Powerplant
two Blackburn Cirrus
Minor II 4-cylinder
inverted air-cooled
in-line piston engines
(75kW/100hp each)

Propellers
two-bladed fixed-pitch
airscrews

PERFORMANCE

Max. speed
130kn (240km/h, 150mph)

Cruise speed
110kn (210km/h, 130mph)

Stall speed
30kn (56km/h, 35mph)

Service ceiling
13,500ft

Rate of climb
870ft/min

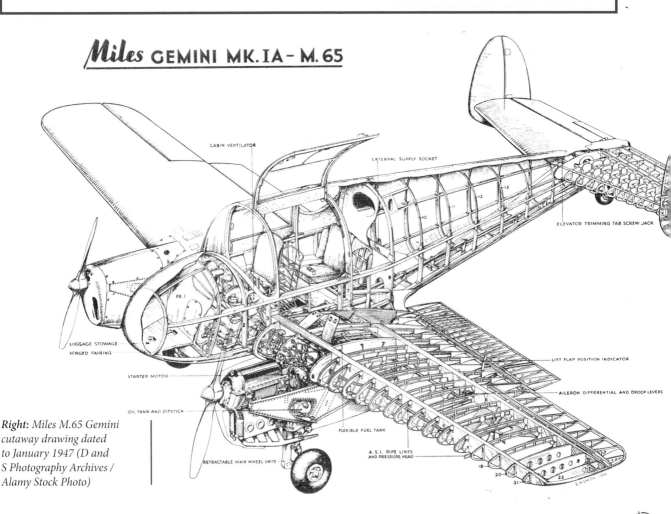

Miles GEMINI MK. IA - M. 65

*Right: Miles M.65 Gemini
cutaway drawing dated
to January 1947 (D and
S Photography Archives /
Alamy Stock Photo)*

As MAF's founders pondered how to commission post-war aircraft to serve isolated communities, their overriding questions were: which missionaries most needed an air service and where were they based?

Below, top: The Miles Gemini at Croydon Aiport, 13 January 1948

Below, bottom: The Miles Gemini's front wheel sunk into the ground, Bulapé

Opposite page, top: The 'Mildmay Pathfinder' on survey in Africa 1948. Refuelling from tins at Kassala in Eastern Sudan, en route to Ethiopia

Opposite page, bottom: Crash of the 'Mildmay Pathfinder' in the Burundi mountains

In 1947, a newly formed MAF set off around the UK, rallying support to buy a plane and launch a survey from London to Africa. Many who encountered MAF on this first UK tour are still part of the MAF family today.

The aircraft of choice, a Miles Gemini, was a new design with twin engines, good visibility and sizeable flaps making it ideal for missionary use. A date in January was settled for departure and a crew was formed comprising Jack Hemmings as pilot, Stuart King as engineer and Tom Banham as navigator. However, in their final weeks of planning, the team realised the Gemini would only have power to carry two passengers. Humbly, Tom Banham departed by sea, headed for Nairobi in Kenya to set up MAF's planning base for the ten-month mission.

Finally, on a cold, blustery day on 13 January 1948, the Gemini – nicknamed 'Mildmay Pathfinder' – sat waiting for departure at Croydon airport, with Jack at the controls and Stuart beside him.

With a 4,000-mile journey ahead and nothing more than a map and compass as their guide, the pair had little idea that this flight would launch a global organisation that would span more than 20 countries and continue for over seven decades.

Their route was planned in short legs of no more than 500 miles, stopping across France at Paris, Marseilles and Corsica and then on to Africa, stopping in Tunis, Tunisia. A further series of short stages took them along the coast of north Africa to Cairo in Egypt, where they discarded the map in favour of following the White Nile as far as the border with Sudan.

Finally, after 26 days, the Gemini arrived in Kenya. From the MAF base in Nairobi, where they reunited with Tom, Jack and Stuart began a series of fights which took them across central Africa, covering the Belgian Congo (now the Democratic Republic of the Congo or DRC), Kenya, the area then known as French Equatorial Africa, Rwanda, Burundi and Tanganyika (now part of Tanzania). For six months, they met mission groups to explore whether aircraft could assist their work, also assessing whether airstrips could be built and government permissions obtained.

A SOFT LANDING

A telegram from Dr Mark Poole in remote Bulapé, in the modern-day DRC, read: 'I'll make you an airstrip if you'll come and land here.' Pulling out thousands of trees to make a landing place, before the days of MAF's own purpose-built airstrips, Dr Poole welcomed the first aircraft ever to land in Bulapé. Jack touched down on soft soil, sinking up to the Gemini's axles. Getting back out involved Jack taking off alone and Dr Poole driving Stuart and their kit 90 miles over appalling roads to meet the plane. The Gemini's small wheels were far from ideal for such adventures.

Sadly, on 10 June 1948, 143 days after its departure from Croydon, the Mildmay Pathfinder made its final flight.

Climbing slowly through the rising valleys of the Burundi foothills, Jack needed 8,500 feet to clear the mountain ahead. A strong headwind generated a downdraught, which quickly converted their climb into a sink rate of 350 feet per minute, at full throttle. Turning the Gemini away, Jack realised they were going down. A banana tree clipped nine inches off the right wing and the aircraft met the dusty mountain.

After a long journey home, Jack and Stuart sat in front of a rather frosty Mildmay Council to present their report. Despite the loss of their aircraft, the council eventually agreed that MAF should try setting up an air service in the vast marshes of southern Sudan. On receiving insurance money for the Gemini, the mission was launched with a ten-seater DH Dragon Rapide, and God opened the next chapter in MAF's history. ✝

> The war had accustomed us to crashes, disasters and the unexpected. But this was different. This wrecked plane was not one of thousands of military aircraft. It was the only one we had. Its broken remains symbolised our shattered hopes.
>
> **Extract from *Hope Has Wings*, Stuart King, 2004, p66**

THE BUS TO NAIROBI

Overland Travel in 1948, an account by MAF co-founder and former Fleet Air Arm navigator Tom Banham en route to Nairobi, Kenya:

When trains run once a week and roads in the wet season sometimes take a days operation, travel plans have to be very elastic in Kenya.

On 31 March 1948 I left for Kangundo, Kenya. It had rained overnight, so the local bus did not leave until 4.30pm. The vehicle was, as usual, completely full of locals and I had the honoured position beside the driver.

Before long, it was evident the journey was going to be interesting. Soon the road became bog and a cross-country detour had to be made. I learned great respect for our driver.

We began to climb a range of hills and I could not believe we would make it. Grinding along in low gear, we strained and twisted over ruts and ridges, between cuts scored by rainwater a foot deep. After a couple of miles the radiator was boiling, so a two-gallon can was produced from the bowels of the bus to refill it.

We approached a gully, a few hundred yards ahead, where the road followed a hairpin bend, a narrow bridge and steep climb. Just before the bend, the earth had been washed away from the rocks underneath the road, so we were driving over the shoulders of huge boulders. Why the bus didn't tip over into the gully is still a mystery to me. It is a rather precarious business with a bus that is full of people and the roof loaded up with the indescribable treasures dear to someone's heart.

HARRY HARTWIG

Harry Hartwig was the first pilot to survey the northern half of Australia with a view to determining the areas most in need.

In the mid 1940s a small group of Christian airmen returning to civilian life met together at a Bible college in Melbourne. They discussed the possibility of using their wartime military training to provide an air service to remote area missions. This led to the founding of Missionary Aviation Fellowship in Australia – although at the outset, it was not even clear which areas most needed the services of such an operation.

By 1949 a Tiger Moth had been procured and, crewed by Harry Hartwig and Alex Freind, this aircraft was used to survey the northern half of Australia with a view to determining the areas most in need. This was followed by a second survey in what was then the Territory of New Guinea. It was decided the greatest need was in what is now Papua New Guinea (PNG) and a base was established at Madang on the country's north coast. The Lutheran Mission was to be the major user of the service and they agreed to cover the cost of an Auster Autocar aircraft and equipment, with MAF providing aircrew and engineering support.

Harry Hartwig was the first pilot and he took up residence in April 1951 with operations beginning early the following month. It was a promising start with many hours of flying logged over the next three months. However, late in the afternoon of Monday 6 August, the aircraft was reported overdue back from a day's flying in the Highlands.

The fate of the radio-less aircraft and its pilot might have forever remained a mystery, had a New Guinean schoolteacher at a mission outpost near the Asaroka Gap not seen an aircraft that afternoon circling in and out of cloud, before hearing an impact on the mountain. Immediately he despatched two boys to carry the message to Asaroka, but it would still be another 1½ days before the aircraft and the body of its pilot was located, 300 feet below the Gap. Not long before, Harry had written the prophetic comment in a report: 'A local knowledge of the weather and topography is essential, and familiarisation flights will be of great value in this respect.'

The loss of the first pilot and plane after just three months of operation was a huge blow. Lacking in both financial and human resources, MAF in Australia turned to MAF USA for assistance. This led to a re-survey of the island and buying a new Cessna 170 aircraft, which was assembled in MAF's hangar in Madang. Operations began again in 1952 with ex-USAAF Pilot Charlie Mellis at the helm. As other missions saw the impact of the MAF service, demand increased, and further bases were opened away from the coast and closer to the areas of need.

Contributing in no small way to the expansion of MAF services in the Territory of New Guinea at the time was a keen and like-minded group of supporters in New Zealand. As early as 1947, a committee had been formed by Murray Kendon and Trevor Strong, with a view to exploring how MAF NZ could best advance the same objectives that were driving the MAF organisations in Australia, the USA and the UK. In time, many of MAF's field staff, both pilots and engineers, would come from across New Zealand. ✈

THE FLEET:
AUSTER AUTOCAR

Aircraft operating in 'hot and high' conditions would require more power.

Just like MAF groups elsewhere around the globe, the fledgling MAF Australia had investigated a range of aircraft types to determine the most suitable for bush operations. Like in the UK, twin-engined aircraft were initially favoured for the safety margins that the additional engine afforded.

An ageing Avro Anson twin was purchased in 1948, but the plan to use this for survey work in New Guinea and Borneo was derailed by the discovery of structural problems with the aircraft's wooden wings. A year later, a tiny de Havilland DH.82 Tiger Moth trainer aircraft was

acquired for use in a survey of remote parts of northern Australia; while acceptable for this purpose, the cramped open-cockpit biplane was far from ideal for a genuine mission aircraft. Eventually the Auster

> ## ❝
> **These earlier aircraft had served successfully as Army cooperation aircraft during World War II, demonstrating their ruggedness and suitability as bush aircraft.**

J/5 Autocar emerged as the favoured choice, largely due to the prohibitive cost of American designs at the time, as well as the Auster's excellent spares availability in Australia.

A four-seater development of earlier two- and three-seater designs, the Autocar had its roots in the pre-war Taylorcraft designs. These earlier aircraft had served successfully as Army cooperation aircraft during World War II, demonstrating their ruggedness and suitability as bush aircraft. The Autocar's performance was adequate but not wonderful; with only the 130hp de Havilland Gipsy Major I

Right: An Auster Autocar, G-AJYK

Opposite: *PNG stamp commemorating fifty years of MAF*

GENERAL CHARACTERISTICS

Crew
one

Capacity
three passengers

Length
7.06m (23ft 2in)

Wingspan
10.97m (36ft)

Height
2.31m (7ft 7in)

Wing area
17.2m² (185sq. ft)

Empty weight
641kg (1,413lb)

Gross weight
1,111kg (2,450lb)

Powerplant
one de Havilland Gipsy
Major I (97kW/130hp)

Propeller
two-bladed fixed-pitch

PERFORMANCE

Max. speed
101kn (187km/h, 116mph)

Cruise speed
87kn (160km/h, 100mph)

Stall speed
30kn (55km/h, 34mph)

Range
430nmi (800km, 500mi)

Service ceiling
11,000ft

Rate of climb
525ft/min

engine fitted, it was recognised by Auster that aircraft operating in 'hot and high' conditions would require more power.

This marginal performance with the Gipsy Major engine was of real concern to MAF Pilot Harry Hartwig; once actually put into service, the aircraft struggled to reach its advertised ceiling of 11,000ft with a 650lb payload and the climb rate was a very disappointing 350ft/min. These figures were only just good enough for operating safely in New Guinea, so when word reached the team that Auster were offering an alternative motor (a 155hp Blackburn Cirrus Major III) for operations in tropical regions, Hartwig was

determined to obtain one at the first opportunity.

Tragically, however, Hartwig was to lose his life attempting to cross the Asaroka Pass in the Central New Guinea Highlands before any upgrades could be made to the aircraft. Commenting in the days following the accident, Stuart King reflected on his

own experiences with the underpowered Miles Gemini in Africa, and ascribed the loss of Harry Hartwig to '... an aircraft unable to produce sufficient reserves of power at high altitude...'. MAF Australia, like MAF UK, would eventually find the solution to this issue in modern all-metal Cessna aircraft. ✈

MAF acquires de Havilland Rapide aircraft, commissioned for **Sudan**

MAF **Sudan** programme launched

MAF **Papua New Guinea** (PNG) programme launched and **Christian Radio Missionary Fellowship** (CRMF) begins

First flights from **Sudan** into **Ethiopia**

MAF **Papua**, Indonesia programme launched

Survey of **Brazil**

Nate Saint begins survey flights over Waodani territory, **Ecuador**

1950   **1951**   **1952** **1953** **1954**   **1955**

2

THE 1950s

With surveys in Africa and South America proving the desperate need for a flight service, MAF began to put down its roots.

MAF ambassadors spread the word of its early successes and news of MAF's pioneering mission began to spread across the world.

As new opportunities opened in Asia Pacific and central Africa, surveys were launched and relationships formed with missionaries living in isolation for the sake of Christ.

The story of the martyrs in Ecuador hit international headlines, touching hearts with a message of hope and forgiveness that was being flown on the wings of MAF planes.

MAF **Brazil** programme launched under affiliate name Asas de Socorro

MAF Pilot Nate Saint martyred by the Waodani tribe in **Ecuador**

Single-engined Cessna 180 aircraft arrives in **Sudan**

Survey of **Ethiopia**

MAF **Kenya** programme launched

1956　　　　　　**1957**　**1958**　**1959**

JUNGLE PILOT

The story of MAF Pilot Nate Saint and his colleagues is one that continues to fuel our mission today; many of our staff cite Nate's life as an inspiration.

Below, left:
Nate and Marj Saint with their children Steve and Kathy, circa 1954

Below, right:
Nate Saint in Ecuador with the Piper

Opposite, top - bottom: Nate Saint with a member of the Waodani tribe; The PA-14 takes off

In the mid-1950s Nate Saint and four American missionary friends felt called to share the Gospel with the Waodani people in Ecuador, an isolated tribe known for their violence against both their own people and outsiders who entered their territory.

Nate and his fellow missionaries – Jim Elliot, Peter Fleming, Ed McCully and Roger Youderian – made first contact with the widely-feared tribe deep in the Ecuadorian rainforest in 1955. Lowering down gifts in a bucket from the plane, every week for 13 weeks, the missionaries hoped to show love and peace to people renowned for violence.

The Waodani had never been contacted by the outside world so it was very exciting.

The tribe not only received their gifts but gradually became more and more accustomed to the arrival of the plane. By the sixth week, tribesmen even attached a beautifully-feathered crown as a return gesture. From then on, gifts were exchanged back and forth until Nate made plans to land.

The group landed on a sandy area they had termed 'Palm Beach' on 3 January 1956, setting up camp on the fringes of Waodani territory, waiting for an encounter.

After three days a group of Waodani appeared on the bank of the river opposite Palm Beach. Jim Elliot waded towards them, his open hand offering a warm invitation for the visitors to join them for food. After a few minutes, all were relaxed and the little group ate hamburgers and drank lemonade.

When their visitors finally disappeared back into the forest, the five friends could barely contain their excitement. This meeting was the one thing they had longed and prayed for.

Two days later, Nate's final call to his wife Marjorie said, 'Pray for us. This is the day!'

At 12 minutes past 3 on Sunday 8 January 1956, Nate's wristwatch was suddenly smashed against a stone. The hands stopped moving.

This is believed to be the moment he and his friends lost their lives to Waodani spears.

Their sudden deaths shocked the world; however, far from

COLUMBIA

Palm Beach

ECUADOR

PERU

being the end of the story, this was just the beginning of their legacy.

Nate's sister, Rachel Saint and Elisabeth Elliot, the wife of Jim, vowed to continue the work that had been started. They were able to make peaceful contact with the men who had killed their brother and husband. Eventually the women went to live with them in the jungle bringing them God's Word, teaching them to forgive fearlessly and love tremendously – transforming their way of life forever.

As a result of their work there was a decline in violence among tribe members; numbers were already very low as a result of 'revenge killing' sprees and there was a possibility that the Waodani may have wiped out their entire population, if not for the outside influence.

At the time of his death, Nate's son Steve was not quite five years old. As he grew up, he spent summers living with his aunt in the jungle where he, too, developed friendships with many members of the tribe. In 1965, he was baptised by two of his father's killers, in the river in which his father had been killed. ✛

> " People who do not know the Lord ask why in the world we waste our lives as missionaries. They forget that they, too, are expending their lives... and when the bubble has burst, they will have nothing of eternal significance to show for the years they have wasted."
>
> **Nate Saint**
> MAF Pilot

THE FLEET:
PIPER FAMILY CRUISER

Effective, adaptable and easy to maintain... ideal for operating from short jungle airstrips.

For many MAF supporters, the image of a bright yellow Piper PA-14 Family Cruiser is forever linked to the shocking events of 8 January 1956: the martyring of five missionaries as they sought to reach the isolated Waodani people of Ecuador. Known as '56-Henry' from its callsign, the little Piper flown by MAF's Nate Saint had made the operation possible, allowing the team to overcome impenetrable jungle and make first contact with the Waodani.

Replacing an older Stinson Voyager aircraft, destroyed by a take-off accident in late 1948 that had left Nate Saint seriously injured, the Piper proved to be effective, adaptable,

— " —

The Piper PA-14 boasted a powerful Lycoming O-235-C1 engine to cope with the increased weight and payload.

and easy to maintain. With it, the small team based at Shell Mera, Ecuador, established a flight operation that was a real benefit to the various mission groups operating in the area. Saint experimented with new, innovative ways of utilising the Piper, including the 'bucket-drop' technique, in which the aircraft was flown in a spiral pattern while lowering a bucket on a long line – a technique which was central to the later operation to reach the Waodani.

Right: Nate Saint maintains the Piper Family Cruiser. Shell Mera, circa 3rd January 1954

Opposite: Steve Saint watches take-off. Shell Mera, circa 1955

⚒ FACTFILE

GENERAL CHARACTERISTICS

Crew
one

Capacity
three passengers

Length
7.06m (23ft 2in)

Wingspan
10.82m (35ft 6in)

Height
1.96m (6ft 5in)

Wing area
16.66m² (179.⅓sq. ft)

Empty weight
463kg (1,020lb)

Gross weight
839kg (1,850lb)

Powerplant
one Lycoming O-235-C1
(86kW/115hp)

Propeller
two-blade Sensenich
fixed-pitch

PERFORMANCE

Max. speed
10kn (198km/h, 123mph)

Cruise speed
96kn (180km/h, 110mph)

Stall speed
38kn (71km/h, 44mph)

Range
434nmi (803km, 499mi)

Service ceiling
12,500ft

Rate of climb
575ft/min

The aircraft was also fitted with an experimental fuel supply system, to provide a back-up in the case of a failed carburettor and even trialled with auxiliary wings to increase its useful load.

The Family Cruiser design was Piper's response to the successful lightweight four-seat designs being marketed by its competitors. First flown in March 1947 and a descendant of their legendary J-3 Cub that was an ultra-basic two-seat monoplane which had been enormously effective in both civilian and military applications, the Family Cruiser boasted a powerful Lycoming O-235-C1 engine, in order to cope with the increased weight and payload. It also had slotted flaps to aid with low-speed manoeuvrability, a feature that was of great benefit when operating from short jungle airstrips and which undoubtedly assisted Nate Saint's 'bucket-drop' technique.

Stripped of fabric by the Waodani, '56-Henry' was abandoned and completely hidden by storms and shifting sands within just a week of the killings. In 1994, nearly forty years after it disappeared, the aircraft was miraculously rediscovered by the Waodani people after flooding had disturbed the sands once more. The surprisingly well-preserved structure was subsequently recovered and is now on display at MAF USA's headquarters in Nampa, Idaho. ✈

COUNTRY PROFILE:
SOUTH SUDAN

With a harsh, tropical climate and only a handful of passable roads, it was the River Nile that pointed Stuart King and Jack Hemmings to land in Sudan – the heart of Africa – in 1948. Using little more than a flimsy, post-war Miles Gemini aircraft, a map and a compass, the pair began to unlock the unseen needs of some of Africa's forgotten people.

Since carving out the first MAF airstrip in 1950, MAF planes have been serving Sudan's poorest people ever since, with only a few years during the late 1960s and early 1970s when MAF operations were forced to cease due to civil war.

The bloody divide between the Islamic/Arabic north and the Christian/animist south has spanned the second half of the Twentieth Century and cost millions of lives. In January 2011, a peaceful referendum backed full independence. Six months later, South Sudan became the world's newest nation.

After just two years, ethnic and political differences, which South Sudanese tribes put aside in the struggle for independence, rapidly reappeared. Ferocious civil war erupted in 2013 and international mediation efforts have yet to deliver a universally acceptable ceasefire.

In 2016, the United Nations (UN) called the situation in South Sudan 'one of the world's worst humanitarian crises of our time'. A third of the population have been forced to flee from their homes, many seeking safety in vast refugee settlements in neighbouring Uganda. Almost five million people are in urgent need of help including over a million children suffering acute malnutrition. Amid reports of widespread looting, sexual violence and recruitment of child soldiers, it's thought that close to 400,000 people have been killed in the recent conflict.

Intensive efforts by aid agencies have so far prevented hunger from turning to famine but, in a country awash with weapons from decades of war, these workers are frequently attacked while trying to deliver relief by road. For many, MAF is the only way to travel in safety.

MAF multiplies the effectiveness of those it flies, reducing days of overland travel to just a few hours. Non-governmental organisations (NGOs) bring aid, development, basic healthcare and a message of Christian compassion to those in acute need, benefitting tens of thousands of people.

For over 70 years, MAF's mission stays unchanged – to reach South Sudan's remotest and poorest communities with the help, hope and healing they need to survive. ✚

> ❝
> **Since carving out the first MAF airstrip in 1950, MAF planes have been serving Sudan's poorest people ever since.**

Main: Lohutok, South Sudan

Above: 5X-MON

Right: A view of the Medair clinic surrounded by Yusuf Batil refugee camp in Maban

Opposite: Sabet Kuj, In Deed and Truth Ministries

COUNTRY STATS

SOUTH SUDAN

★ Juba

👤 POPULATION
10.2m (excluding 2.3 refugees abroad)

☆ CAPITAL
Juba

💬 LANGUAGES
English, Arabic + 60 indigenous languages

🚩 ROADS
4,350 miles, mostly unpaved (245,000 in the UK)

☀ CLIMATE
Tropical: hot all year round; rains from May to November

〜 LIFE EXPECTANCY
57 years

🚩 MAF AIRSTRIPS
57

🔗 MAF PARTNERS
200+ organisations

✛ FLEET
2 x Cessna 182 SMA
2 x Cessna 208

"MAF's north-eastern weekly shuttle is a huge blessing. Before, we had to drive for hours on a risky road where people get ambushed and shot at. On top of being more secure, we benefit from the fact that it only takes five minutes to drive to our local airstrip."

Sabet Kuj
CEO, In Deed and Truth Ministries

TIMELINE

1948 First MAF survey flight touches down in Sudan

1950 First regular operations begin from Malakal

1956 Independence from Britain

1964 Expulsion of missionaries and closure of MAF programme

1977 Respite in civil war; programme restarts

1983 Operations relocate to Lokichoggio, Kenya due to government restrictions

1992 Relief flights into Sudan continue from Kenya

2003 Relief flights into Sudan from Uganda

2006 New MAF base established in Juba

2008 First pilot family for 25 years arrives

2011 South Sudan becomes the world's newest nation

2015 Cessna 182 SMA joins the fleet

2019 Two additional Cessna Caravans join the fleet; South Sudan becomes MAF's busiest African programme

South Sudan

DE HAVILLAND DH.89 RAPIDE

All struts and wires, the de Havilland DH.89 Rapide biplane was a pre-war design, lacking the sleekness and modernity of the post-war Miles Gemini it replaced in MAF service.

First flown as early as 1934, the Rapide was a product of Britain's legendary de Havilland company and was conceived as a regional passenger aircraft. Pressed into service with the Royal Air Force and Royal Navy during World War II, Rapides were used extensively as communications and training aircraft. Upon reverting to their original role at the end of the war, the Rapides were popular with airline operators and passengers alike, becoming arguably the most successful British-built short-haul commercial passenger aircraft to be produced during the 1930s.

MAF's selection of the Rapide was a more straightforward process than had been the case with the Miles Gemini. With a tight budget, restricted to the insurance settlement from the loss of the Gemini, which crashed, as well as the need

> ## ❝
> **With a relatively spacious cabin and seating for up to eight passengers, the carrying capacity of the Rapide was greatly superior to that of the Gemini.**

to comply with the Sudanese government's refusal to allow single-engined aircraft to operate within their borders, the options were very limited. In Stuart King's own words, 'There weren't too many twin-engined planes we could afford… the only one of reasonable size and price was the veteran de Havilland Rapide.' The twin engines in question were de Havilland's own Gipsy Six inverted-inline engines, each producing 200hp – double the power that the Gemini's Cirrus Minor engines could develop.

The aircraft eventually purchased by MAF had been built for the Royal Air Force as

Right: De Havilland DH.89 Rapide aircraft

Opposite: *Stuart King*

GENERAL CHARACTERISTICS

Crew
one

Capacity
eight passengers

Length
10.5m (34ft 6in)

Overall Wingspan
14.6m (48ft)

Height
3.1m (10ft 3in)

Wing area
32m² (340sq. ft)

Empty weight
1,460kg (3,230lb)

Loaded weight
2,490kg (5,500lb)

Powerplant
two de Havilland Gipsy
Six in-line (149kW/200hp
each)

Propellers
two-bladed fixed-pitch

PERFORMANCE

Max. speed
136kn (253km/h, 157mph)
at 1,000ft

Range
498nmi (920km, 573mi)

Service ceiling
16,700ft

Rate of climb
867ft/min

'There weren't too many twin-engined planes we could afford... the only one of reasonable size and price was the veteran de Havilland Rapide'

Stuart King
MAF co-founder

a DH.89A Dominie I, for training radio operators during the war. It had retained its powerful Marconi radio from that role, something that would be of great benefit in the skies above southern Sudan. With a relatively spacious cabin and seating for up to eight passengers, the carrying capacity of the Rapide was greatly superior to that of the Gemini, allowing MAF to establish an effective and useful air transport service for mission staff in southern Sudan. It is perhaps hard to envisage how this might have been possible if the diminutive Gemini had still been the primary aircraft type in service.

Despite their somewhat archaic appearance, MAF's Rapide aircraft proved to be solid and reliable. In the unforgiving flying conditions of southern Sudan, the ruggedness and simplicity of De Havilland's design was of real benefit, particularly given the limited engineering resources that MAF had at the time. Constructed from timber and skinned largely with fabric, repairs to the aircraft structure relied more on carpentry skills than precision engineering.

Sadly, this wooden construction was also to prove the Rapide's Achilles heel: without effective hangarage, the aircraft were exposed to all that the southern Sudanese climate could throw at them; the fabric skins, structural adhesives and critical wing-spar timbers were all seriously compromised over time. The eventual answer would be a move to more modern all-metal aircraft that would be less vulnerable to variations in temperature and humidity, but the Rapide, for all its quaint 'antique elegance' was a wonderful solution to the huge challenges of pioneering MAF's work in East Africa. ✈

LETTERS FROM THE 1950s

Extract from a letter written by one of MAF's early mission partners, Gospel Recordings, following their first flight from Uganda to Sudan. The group were led to make tape recordings of the Gospel in 57 Sudanese tribal languages.

```
MAF Prayer Letter, August 1955

April 8th, 1955 — Good Friday
```

Long before dawn we listened to a great drama in thunder and lightning with steady rain… it was really a symphony of all kinds of variety. Thunder began like a growl, gathering momentum into a great roar, then crashed splinteringly, suddenly upon us then wandered away, echoing in smaller and smaller replicas of its first voice.

At 7.30am, time of our scheduled flight with MAF, it was soupy with fog and rain. MAF Pilots Gordon Marshall and Alistair Macdonald were advised to wait. So we waited, busy enough with correspondence and coupling record titles in the 57 sets we have in our present catch for Africa.

At 8.55am, we climbed into the silver and red striped de Havilland Rapide. Airborne by 9am, Gordon was at the controls, Alistair at the radio. Leaving the rolling green country and Lake Victoria, we flew northward toward very extensive cloud masses.

We were in and out of clouds and turbulence that tossed our Rapide like a puppet on a string. Alastair talked to us comfortingly through more white invisibility and turbulence. 'These little planes, can they take it?' I asked. 'Oh yes, they are very strong.'

'How far to Malakal?'

'Six hundred and sixty miles as the crow flies.'

Now we are up at 8,500 feet and the most disconcerting turbulence. We soared like a badminton birdie, then dropped! I noticed the tossing, the pressure and Gordon's flush of excitement, tense and silent as he flew the plane. The pilots told us afterwards that it was the worst turbulence they had ever been in.

At last we were out into the clear and descending to a better view of the flat patterns of green below us. Malakal finally sighted… a tiny circular brooch set in a vast land, barren as the surface of the moon, where the silver Nile is sketched all the way to the skyline. This is MAF's headquarters, who are to be our transport and co-ordinators for our entire coverage of Sudan.

Opposite, top to bottom:
Pilot Gordon Marshall delivering part of the Bible in Uduk language, Chali-el-fil, southern Sudan; Gordon Marshall (seated) weighing luggage to be loaded into the Rapide; MAF Hangar at Malakal, 1958; Stuart King (left) and Alastair MacDonald (right) changing the engine on the third Rapide in the Malakal Hangar

July 3rd, 1955

It is breath-taking really to look back on those 2 1/2 months and realise that thousands of miles were covered and recordings obtained, from areas so vastly separated, in 50 languages.

We could have done nothing if it had not been for MAF.

Extract from *Missionary Partners' Letter*, July 1956

The story of our return journey is so different that it is almost ludicrous! We hopped into the eight-seater de Havilland Rapide and were whisked back to our mission base at Akobo, South Sudan. Below us at intervals we could see the Nile snaking its way in a continuous series of U-bends though this desolate prairie land. The plane took us straight to our destination: one and half hours instead of nine days.

In early April we hope to use MAF to survey Annak and Murle country. Such a project done any other way would take many months; with a plane it will be two days. More outstanding figures have been brought to our attention: before MAF, our members would have spent a total of 336 days travelling. Had MAF been available, the same distances would have been covered in 36 hours. One year versus 1 1/2 days!

Extract from *MAF Prayer Letter*, September 1957

One Tuesday morning, two-year-old Loraine was playing outdoors on an isolated mission base in the Nuba Mountains, Sudan. Someone suddenly noticed that she was choking. She had been eating peanuts and evidently one had gone down her windpipe. The nurses on the base did their best to remove it: picked her up by her heels; gave her pepper to make her sneeze; tried in every way to dislodge it but without success. The situation became serious. Her father realised she must be taken to hospital, but the rains were making the roads almost impassable now. The only vehicle was a tractor — but very recently a fellow worker had taken nine days to travel 250 miles. The hospital was even further.

Was the MAF plane nearby?

The nearest telephone was 30 miles away. Realising that the aircraft might not even be at base, he left his little girl with her mother, who was resting after the birth of their new baby just three days previously. By 7pm he reached the phone and made the call. MAF could help.

By first light MAF arrived to pick up little Loraine, her father and a nurse. They were all flown to Khartoum, Sudan, where the child was admitted to hospital. The chest specialist successfully performed the operation and they were flown back to their home shortly afterwards, having been away for only 32 hours.

We give praise to the Lord for the timing of this incident:

- The MAF plane could have been away when the call came

- A dust storm struck Khartoum at 4pm, after MAF had successfully landed. Had it come earlier, they would have had to turn back on their journey

- The only man who could perform the operation left for England the very next day

Bottom: MAF's first landing in Akobo, Nov 1950

Opposite, top to bottom: An easy road compared to many in Africa; Betty Greene in front of MAF's new Cessna 180; Betty Greene with Stuart and Phyllis King leaving with MAF's first Cessna 180 ferry flight to Sudan

Above and Beyond

Extract from *MAF Prayer Letter*, April 1957

At two minutes past ten on Friday 1 March, the new single-engined Cessna plane took off from London Airport, outward bound for Sudan. On board were Betty Greene, the pilot, Stuart King, the engineer/radio operator and his wife, Phyllis King, with their two children.

As the little plane took off on its long flight of 8,000 miles, those who had gathered around to see it off after a word of prayer, were full of praise to God for a beautiful clear day for the first leg over Europe.

'Hi Stuart, this is Harvey Hoekstra. I've got an aeroplane here for you. It's a Cessna 180.'

The plane was four years old and seemed in good shape. Harvey had aroused the interest of a group of Michigan businessmen in the value and needs of MAF. They had put up the money and were ready to buy the plane. But that wasn't the end of the story. Charlie Mellis, the secretary of MAF USA went further:

'Stuart, if you agree, we can sell your second-hand [Rapide] and, because we get such a good discount from the makers, we can then buy you a new one for the same price.'

Miracle upon miracle.

We could have danced for joy.

I've often thought about those two Cessna 180s. The first took two years of persistent prayer and work to obtain. The second came with a flash. We could thank God for both of them, both the provision and timing were in His hands.

Extract from *Hope Has Wings*, Stuart King, 2004, pp164-165

AIRSTRIP OPENING:
WE WILL MAKE A PLACE

An army of Mabaan people rally to clear an airstrip at Doro, South Sudan.

Below, left:
First landing at Doro

Below, right:
Creation of the airstrip at Doro

Opposite:
Gordon Marshall re-fuelling a Cessna 180 at Doro, Upper Nile Province, southern Sudan, watched by the local Mabaan

Herb Major had ridden 125 slow miles on muleback to reach Doro, where a small mission base lay hidden in the top eastern corner of South Sudan. His family, left in Khartoum, would have to wait five months for the dry season before they could join him. Surely there was an alternative?

Mission Leader Dr Malcolm Forsberg – known by everyone as Mal – had invited MAF to inspect the site a few months earlier. Although the ground near Doro mission station was firm enough for a landing, it was covered by thick undergrowth and trees – some 9 metres in diameter and 18 metres high. The trees would have to be burned, and many solid, three-metre-high termite hills removed.

With only a few tools at the mission centre, Herb would have to persuade the local Mabaan people to help.

Before it was ready, well over 1,000 people toiled on the airstrip, gathering from many surrounding villages to help.

The early morning flight from Khartoum with Mal, Herb's wife Mary Ethel and their two small children began a special era for Stuart King, who had just received the radio licences to begin MAF's earliest operations with their de Havilland Rapide aircraft.

Finding the airstrip at Doro in the featureless expanse of

" For the next seven years, the radio operator's compartment became my home in the plane. During many difficult landings and take offs, I'd find I was either praying us safely down or praying us safely up. I kept an eye on the passengers and provided them with tea from a Thermos, always enjoying giving a good cabin service.

'We had to get the people excited enough about the coming of a plane to work on the airstrip,' wrote Mal in 1950.

'It was hard to explain why the little speck on the horizon needed a long space to sit down when birds did not need much room to land and could sit on the branch of a tree.

'It will bring my wife and babies just as soon as you make a place for it to sit,' explained Herb.

Mabaans had never understood how planes got so high and stayed there. 'How small were the men and women in the planes that were only specks in the sky? You are going to let your wife and children go up there' they implored.

Eventually the chief spoke. 'We will make a place.'

Last Days on the Nile, Mal Forsberg, 1966

grassland with Mal as their guide would not be easy, and Pilot Steve Stevens needed to drop off their passengers at Malakal to make an initial safe landing. After 1¼ hours, they could see nothing of it.

'I'm starting a square search procedure,' called Steve, scanning the unrevealing countryside below.

After some time, 'There's the strip,' he called. A smoke fire burned to show wind direction, and the three men tightened their belts for landing.

Narrowly missing three goats, which darted onto the airstrip in fear of the engine, Steve brought the plane down smoothly on the excellently-prepared strip. Herb was first at the cabin door with crowds of Mabaans clutching their spears behind him. 'I have never been so excited in all my life!' he beamed.

The Mabaans were excited too, seeing a plane on the ground for a first time, much larger than they could ever have imagined. They looked closely at the men who emerged from within – these foolhardy people who travelled in such a strange and dangerous vehicle.

The return flight a few days later on 4 December, safely reunited Herb with Mary Ethel and their children. 'It gave us great satisfaction to see the Major family reunited,' reflected Stuart King. 'God was good. Our regular operations had made a very positive start!' ✈

COUNTRY PROFILE:
PAPUA NEW GUINEA

The Independent State of Papua New Guinea (PNG) forms the eastern half of the island of New Guinea and is home to more indigenous groups than many places on Earth. Rugged mountains, active volcanoes, dense jungles and extensive swamplands dominate the country's landscape, making it almost impossible for remote groups to interact with one another.

Many communities are reliant on subsistence farming due to the high cost of developing infrastructure in such a harsh terrain. This means almost 80% of the population are prevented from accessing the resources they need to break free from poverty.

The sheer logistical challenge of overland travel has resulted in over 800 indigenous languages being spoken across the country – making PNG the most linguistically-diverse nation in the world. This isolation, diversity and vulnerability presents a perfect landscape for MAF's vision of reaching isolated people with help, hope and healing.

In the early 1950s, Christianity had become the dominant religion in PNG. MAF was valuable to the growth of a strong Church, supporting missionaries who planted churches, built Bible schools and shared the Gospel message in remote Highland villages. Today, it's thought that almost 95% of people in PNG identify themselves as Christians, however, tensions prevail between Biblical values and the animist practices of indigenous tribes who continue to blame evil spirits for sickness, misfortune or death.

PNG is now MAF's busiest programme, recognised by the government, international aid agencies and local communities as a vital, safe service and a reliable way to travel. MAF has made a conscious commitment to the long-term development of the country by employing and training around 100 local staff.

Because so many people are dependent on aviation to access basic provisions, maintaining the airstrip network is an urgent priority. In 2013, MAF founded the Rural Airstrip Agency (RAA), which has become a separate NGO and works with the government and communities to restore airstrips and develop new landing sites. When an MAF aircraft touches down for the first time, pilots are greeted with cheering, clapping, singing and dancing – signs of how much a new airstrip means to those living nearby.

For many indigenous groups, MAF has provided the first opening to medicine, technology, education and the Good News of Christ. MAF's role has changed over the years, firstly supporting individual missionaries and now sustaining entire communities. By flying food to market, delivering building equipment, transporting teachers and carrying out medical evacuations (medevacs), villages have been transformed, modernised and connected with the outside world. ✠

Above: Aerial view of April River airstrip

Right: Karina Mills, Kompian District Hospital

Opposite: MAF PNG pilot Irwin Hodder at Tifilimin picking up vegetables and passenger to fly to the MAF base at Tabubil

COUNTRY STATS

PAPUA NEW GUINEA

★ Port Moresby

AUSTRALIA

👤 **POPULATION**
7.3 million

☆ **CAPITAL**
Port Moresby

💬 **LANGUAGES**
English, Tok Pisin
+ 830 indigenous
languages

🚩 **ROADS**
5,809 miles, mostly
unpaved (245,000
in the UK)

☀ **CLIMATE**
Tropical; monsoon
rains December to
March

🩺 **LIFE EXPECTANCY**
67.5 years

🚩 **MAF AIRSTRIPS**
211

🔗 **MAF PARTNERS**
36 organisations

✛ **FLEET**
9 x Cessna 208

"Without MAF, we wouldn't be able to run our hospital."

Karina Mills
Kompiam District
Hospital

TIMELINE

○ **1951** MAF air operations begin

○ **1956** Technology Services launched (known locally as CRMF)

○ **1960s** Operations expand throughout the Highlands and into the lowland and coastal regions

○ **1962** Airstrip completed and supply route opens to support mission at Oksapmin and Telefomin

○ **1975** PNG gains independence from Australia

○ **1997** Government declares national state of disaster following prolonged drought. Hundreds die and 1.2 million risk starvation

○ **2005** Critical shortage of skilled pilots and aircraft maintenance engineers threatens MAF's ministry

○ **2013** Rural Airstrip Agency (RAA) begins work in partnership with MAF

○ **2015** Drought and frost decimates sweet potato crop in Highlands. MAF provides relief flights to distribute emergency food

○ **2017** New Cessna Caravan joins the fleet, increasing capacity to 12 aircraft

○ **2018** Powerful earthquakes strike country's Highlands causing widespread disaster. MAF is a key aerial responder

Papua New Guinea

CHRISTIAN RADIO MISSIONARY FELLOWSHIP (CRMF)

A group of men returned to Australia from WWII with their own vision of using military-learned skills to proclaim the Gospel.

Beginning with children's Bible stories, Claude D'Evelynes, Syd McLeod-Jones and Bob Hartnell set up a radio transceiver, which broadcast the Gospel to radio stations and portable short-wave transmitters used by missionaries across Australia and New Zealand. Shortly after, a high-frequency (HF) radio network was established.

By the early 1950s, it became clear that the people of PNG were in need of a quality, reliable communications network. Initially, the team set up a hydro-electric power station to transmit radio from Rugli in the country's Western Highlands, establishing PNG's own HF network. For around 40 years, radio was broadcast from Rugli, under the name Christian Radio Mission Fellowship (CRMF)

and hundreds of remote peoples heard about Jesus Christ.

MAF flew CRMF technicians, who installed radios in very remote villages across PNG.

— ❝ —

Even in the early years, CRMF and MAF worked closely to reach remote communities with the Gospel.

In 1993, CRMF moved to Goroka, PNG and the team broadcast from a Salvation Army hall until a purpose-built Communications Centre was completed in 2001. CRMF was among the first technical providers to develop an HF radio email system for amateur-band radio.

With growing operations,

an extension was added to the Communications Centre in 2009 and a Learning Technologies initiative was launched in 2010 – a project deploying Bible training and resources to remote communities through the use of various new technologies, including Wi-Fi, mobile phone networks and both audio and printed Bibles. In the same year, CRMF officially became an MAF ministry, amalgamating under a memorandum of understanding in May and becoming known as Technology Services, PNG.

Today, CRMF's vision is to fulfil the communication and technical needs of the Church, serving remote communities throughout PNG so that every tribe and indigenous group can hear about the Good News of Jesus in a language they understand. ✛

Main: Papua New Guinea, home of CRMF

Opposite, top to bottom: *Claude D'Evelynes, Syd McLeod-Jones and Bob Hartnell in the early 1950s; Amila; CRMF radio equipment*

MAF NEWS

CRMF received a radio call from a remote community in Hela Province, PNG. Alima, a 14-year-old girl had been chopping firewood and lacerated three of her toes. She was bleeding badly and in a critical condition, but she was miles from a medical clinic. The CRMF radio operator contacted MAF and requested an urgent medevac flight – although the family couldn't afford for Alima's father to travel with her and MAF couldn't allow Alima to fly unaccompanied. Time was running out and Alima needed urgent surgery. All the family could do was pray.

Thanks to the emergency medevac fund and the vital HF radio network in Alima's village, MAF was able to subsidise the cost of an extra ticket and fly both Alima and her father to Rumginae Hospital.

Alima's family and relatives are thankful to God for MAF, CRMF and the generosity of God's Kingdom.

Joy Suarkia, CRMF story, 26 July 2019

> HF radio email later became called Winlink Global Radio Email, used by NGOs and governments to transmit weather bulletins, emergency and relief communications across very remote locations.

MAF IN THE AMERICAS

From Betty Greene's inaugural MAF flight transporting two Wycliffe workers to Tuxpan, Mexico in 1946, MAF's work in the Americas has continued to evolve and expand throughout its history.

Main: XB-GGU (Cessna 206) on an airstrip, Mexico

Below: Betty Greene next to Waco Duck, Peruvian Jungle. circa 1950

Opposite: TG-BAY takes off, Guatemala

Launching an operation in Ecuador in 1948 under the name *Alas de Socorro* (Wings of Help), MAF hit international headlines when Nate Saint and four other missionaries were martyred, eight years later.

The men were honoured by the President of Ecuador, who conferred upon them the National Medal of Merit in the Order of Commander. Ecuador later issued five commemorative stamps, each picturing one of the missionaries.

Christian ministry has continued among the Waodani people, and the story of the Palm Beach martyrs has been retold through film, documentary and in print. The Saint family's moving testimony of faith and forgiveness has raised awareness of MAF's international mission across the globe.

To date, MAF has operated aircraft in 13 countries across Latin America, now having handed much of the management to local people, who have caught the vision to serve isolated communities in their own countries with God's love. ✠

MAF'S JOURNEY IN THE AMERICAS

○ **1946 Feb** MAF's first flight to Mexico, piloted by Betty Greene

○ **1946 July** Betty Greene arrives in Peru to support SIL by flying their amphibious Grumman 'Duck'. She becomes the first woman to fly over the Andes mountains.

○ **1947 May** Operation launched in Chiapas, Mexico with a Piper Cruiser aircraft

○ **1947** MAF survey of Ecuador completed

○ **1948 Sept** Operations launched in Ecuador (under the name Alas de Socorro)

○ **1949** Three regions surveyed in Colombia

○ **1950** Hobey Lowrance surveys Honduras and Venezuela in a Piper Clipper aircraft, covering over 110,000 square miles of uncharted territory

○ **1951 Nov** Operations launched in Honduras (ceased in 1996)

○ **1954 June** Two-year survey of all Brazilian regions served by mission groups

○ **1955 Sept** Nate Saint spots the first Waodani village from the air, beginning 13 weeks of aerial contact and gifts being dropped

○ **1956 Jan** Nate Saint and his companions are martyred on Palm Beach

○ **1958** Operations launched in Brazil (under the name Asas de Socorro)

○ **1959** MAF opens a maintenance centre in Brazil

○ **1960 Oct** Operations launched in British Guiana (now Guyana) by Roy Parsons

○ **1963 May** Operations launched in Dutch Guiana (now Suriname) by Roy and Katie Parsons

○ **1964 Oct** Operations launched in Puerto Ayacucho, Venezuela by Chuck Bennett and Don Roberson (ceased 2006)

○ **1965 Oct** Queen Juliana of the Netherlands personally visits MAF Suriname and dedicates the Cessna 185 Flying Dutchman

○ **1966 Sept** Nate Saint's children are baptised by the same Waodani who killed their father ten years earlier

○ **1971 Feb** Operations launched in Colombia by Jack Walker using a Cessna 180 aircraft (ceased in 1987)

○ **1972 Aug** Operations launched in Nicaragua by Dan and Jerri Merrill (ceased in 1996)

○ **1977** Operations launched in Guatemala

○ **1986 Nov** Alas de Socorro becomes a national entity in Ecuador. MAF continue to manage, staff, and provide funding

○ **1994 Jun** Bill Clapp locates the remains of Nate Saint's plane in Ecuador

○ **1999** MAF staff transition out of Guatemala as the operation becomes an affiliate named AGAPE

○ **2000** Management of operations in Mexico and Suriname transition to local boards, becoming two affiliate programmes

○ **2006** MAF launches a Village Radio Project to install radio communication in at least 70 remote villages of Ecuador

○ **2009** In Ecuador, MAF hands over management of operations to a local board of directors

XB-GGU

REACHING THE LACANDÓN PEOPLE

Pilot John Strash recalls early memories of reaching Mexico's Lacandón people with the Gospel:

Linguist and anthropologist Phillip Baer and his wife Mary lived among the Lacandón people in the southern state of Chiapas near the Mexican/Guatemalan border. They were working for Wycliffe Bible Translators with a desire to show the love of Jesus Christ to the indigenous group.

In the spring of 1957 Obregon, a Lacandón Chief, invited Phillip and Mary Baer to move to his village at Ixtelja. 'We want to read and write,' he said. Accepting the invitation, the Baer family began the day's trek through the jungle to build an airstrip and set up living accommodation.

When preparations were complete, I flew Mary, their five children, dog, chickens, ducks and all their earthly possessions in several flights to their new home.

A few weeks later, Chief Obregon suffered a severe case of malaria and I was called for an emergency medevac. We loaded Obregon into the MAF plane and took off on the 90-minute flight to a hospital in Tuxtla Gutiérrez. The chief showed no fear of flying as he recognised the jungle trails below, but when we flew over the paved highway, he was perplexed.

'¿Que es esto?' he asked. It was a *camino*, a road, I explained. He had never seen anything like it in his life.

Landing at Tuxtla Gutiérrez, a car awaited. '¿*Que es esto*?' Having only ever travelled by foot or by air, Obregon assumed that this vessel would fly. 'No,' I explained: 'You will ride in this to the hospital, along the road.'

Obregon was the first Lacandón to leave the jungles. Restored to good health, I flew him back to his people at Ixtelja. As a result of our kindness, Obregon volunteered to help with Phillip's Bible translation work, accepting Christ over time. Soon the whole tribe followed. ✝

Below: Piper aircraft at hangar in Mexico

Opposite: *John Strash and Phil Baer*

UNITED STATES OF AMERICA

MEXICO

Chiapas

THE LACANDÓN PEOPLE

The Lacandón are one of the Maya peoples who live in the Lacandón jungles of Chiapas, southern Mexico. They are thought to be one of the most isolated and culturally conservative of Mexico's native peoples and became almost extinct in the 1940s due to a severe yellow fever epidemic.

Traditionally, the tribe worshipped their own gods who they believe dwell in the sky and below the earth. Small ceramic bowls known as 'god pots' were created with the head and face of a deity, filled with incense and considered to be alive and have a soul. Through friendship with Christian missionaries, the southern Lacandón abandoned their pantheon of gods and turned to Christ, working with Phillip and Mary Baer to translate the Bible into their own language.

Today, the Lacandón population has grown significantly to roughly 1,000 and various institutions are devoted to helping them cope with the changes imposed by recent times. Development of roads and new, modern villages along with acute deforestation have threatened traditional Lacandón principles. The Lacandón were forced from dispersed settlements to more centralised communities. Economic practices have begun to encompass the growing tourist trade, which flows into the area. Many Lacandón have now decided to earn a living in the huge logging industry and strategies to withdraw back into the forest have widely been abandoned for modern ways of living.

LOCATION PROFILE:
PAPUA

Papua – formerly known as Dutch New Guinea and Irian Jaya – is the largest and most easterly province of Indonesia, a cluster of islands in the Indian Ocean.

Located on the western half of New Guinea, Papua is bordered by PNG to the east and shares a similar landscape dominated by mountains and jungles. More than 250 ethnic groups are enclosed within its almost impenetrable terrain.

Home to Indonesia's highest mountain peak, Puncak Jaya, one of the world's Seven Summits, it is considered by some to be the most technically challenging mountain to climb on Earth. The peak also encircles the Grasberg – the world's largest gold mine – yet Papuans comprise the poorest sector of Indonesian society.

During the late 1950s, demand for MAF's work grew rapidly when Marjorie Saint – the wife of martyred missionary Nate Saint – toured Australia, stirring up support and appetite to reach isolated communities in Asia Pacific.

> **Today Papua is one of MAF's busiest programmes, with more than 1.6 million kilos of cargo being transported annually by 11 aircraft to communities dependent on its vital air service.**

In 1952, former US military Flight Instructor Grady Parrott granted permission to launch MAF's first official survey of Dutch New Guinea. Flying across the untouched Baliem Valley, Grady uncovered the Dani people, in an area most geographers assumed to be unpopulated.

From the earliest stages of the programme, MAF has flown food, medicine and missionary personnel to hidden communities across the province, speeding community development and enabling access to education in areas unreached by the outside world.

With only 3% of Gross Domestic Product (GDP) spent on health care in Indonesia as a whole, there are only 1.2 hospital beds available for every 1,000 people. This leaves much of the population in desperate need of medical assistance. In remote areas, countless Papuans suffer from treatable conditions such as malaria and malnutrition and in some inland areas, HIV and AIDS levels are over 12 times the national average.

MAF's modern flying includes medical emergencies, with pilots transporting patients to hospital from rural villages and even seeing babies born mid-flight.

Today Papua is one of MAF's busiest programmes, with more than 1.6 million kilos of cargo being transported annually by 11 aircraft to communities dependent on its vital air service. In a place with tremendous physical and spiritual needs, the truth of the Gospel, along with practical and medical help assistance, is transforming the lives of vulnerable and isolated people. ✈

Main:
Mountain village, Papua

Below: Papuans in traditional dress at Soba

Right: Baby 'Dennis MAF' safely delivered mid-flight

LOCATION STATS

👤 **POPULATION**
3.35 million

☀ **CLIMATE**
Tropical; hot, humid

☆ **PROVINCIAL CAPITAL**
Jayapura

〰 **LIFE EXPECTANCY**
73.2 years

💬 **LANGUAGES**
Bahasa Indonesia, English, Dutch + 700 indigenous languages

🚩 **MAF AIRSTRIPS**
160

🔗 **MAF PARTNERS**
31 organisations

🚩 **ROADS**
1,457 miles
(245,000 in the UK)

✈ **FLEET**
3 x Cessna 208
3 x Cessna 208B
5 x Quest Kodiak 100

Jayapura

PAPUA

PNG

TIMELINE

○ **1952** Survey flight by Grady Parrott, MAF programme launched

○ **1954** MAF base opens at Sentani

○ **1958** MAF base opens at Nabire

○ **1958** The Dani people, first reached by MAF, embrace the Gospel

○ **1959** The first Dani missionaries reconcile with the tribe and 1,000 come to Christ

○ **1974** MAF base opens at Wamen

○ **2001** MAF base opens at Merauke

○ **2003** MAF base opens at Timika

○ **2012** First flight to the unreached village of Esrotnamba

MAF NEWS

Responding in 2019 to a call for help, MAF Pilot Dennis Bergstrazer flew to Ilaga, a small farming town in a remote mountain valley. There he collected expectant mother Arida who was experiencing a difficult labour and needed hospital assistance.

About halfway to the hospital at Timika, Dennis realised the patient was giving birth. Fortunately, the nurse on board had the necessary equipment to safely deliver a little boy. Dennis, who had taken off with six passengers landed with seven.

The joyful and thankful parents named their newborn son in honour of their pilot and airborne delivery suite – 'Dennis MAF'.

We've worked very closely with MAF throughout the years and we're so thankful. Everything that's happened here is because of what MAF's flight services have offered us. Everything we need, MAF is providing in a very, very good, efficient way."

Stephen Crockett
Missionary working with the Moi people

Papua

THE FLEET:
CESSNA 180

Rugged, reliable and easy to operate.

Arguably MAF's first truly 'modern' aircraft type, the Cessna 180 represented a huge step forward for MAF operations when it was introduced in southern Sudan in 1957. Just like the examples of the model still in use by MAF to this day, the new high-wing, all-metal monoplane design was rugged, reliable, and relatively easy to operate.

Cessna introduced its C180 model in 1953, originally marketing it as 'the businessman's airplane'. However, it quickly gained a reputation for solid dependability and practicality, ultimately proving itself to be a consummate bush-flying aircraft, hugely popular with pilots operating in the harshest of environments. A grand total of 6,193 C180s of varying specifications were built over a 28-year production run; it also spawned a range of successors, including the Cessna 182 SMA which still fills an important role in MAF today.

> ## "
> **The floatplane's ability to reach almost anywhere on the river network was a real benefit to MAF.**

As well as Cessna's solid construction techniques and clean aerodynamics, a big part of the C180's success was down to the powerful, yet compact and reliable Continental O-470 series of flat-six engines.

The four-seater C182s were much smaller aircraft than the de Havilland DH.89 Rapides that they replaced in MAF service. However, despite this apparent disadvantage, the Cessna design proved to be much more appropriate for the needs of MAF, allowing greater adaptability. This flexibility was exemplified by the decision to put one of MAF's two C180s on floats, to better reach communities along the Nile and its tributaries. Described by local people as 'the plane with slippers on', the floatplane's ability to reach almost anywhere on the river network was a real benefit to MAF, as it operated in a region often cut off by floods during the rainy season. ✈

Right: Stuart King (left) with the Cessna 180

Opposite: *Floatplane ideally suited to river networks*

GENERAL CHARACTERISTICS

Crew
one

Capacity
five passengers

Length
7.85m (25ft 9in)

Wingspan
10.92m (35ft 10in)

Height
2.36m (7ft 9in)

Wing area
16.2m² (174sq. ft)

Empty weight
771kg (1,700lb)

Gross weight
1,270kg (2,800lb)

Powerplant
one Continental
O-470-U (170kW/230hp)

Propeller
two-bladed constant-
speed, 2.08m (6ft 10in)
diameter

PERFORMANCE

Max. speed
148kn (274km/h, 170mph)

Cruise speed
142kn (263km/h, 163mph)

Stall speed
48kn (89km/h, 55mph)

Range
890nmi (1,650km, 1,020m)

Service ceiling
17,700ft

Rate of climb
1,100ft/min

The Cesssna 180's powerplant was very different to the British-built engines with which the MAF pioneers were used to working; after the 12-day, 5,000-mile delivery flight of the first C180 aircraft, Stuart King was '...amazed how clean the engine was.

'The inverted cylinders in the Gypsy Queen engines of our old Rapide had spewed oil around on every flight. The Cessna, with its horizontally opposed six-cylinder engine, remained clean. I could have maintained it with white gloves on.'

Hope Has Wings, Stuart King, 2004, p170

COUNTRY PROFILE:
KENYA

The Republic of Kenya takes its name from Mount Kenya, Africa's second highest peak. A melting pot of rich tribal and ethnic cultures, due to relative political stability, Kenya is not only an attractive tourist destination but also a host country for thousands of refugees. However, the semi-arid terrain and inconsistent rainfall cause widespread hunger for millions of people who rely on agriculture to survive. Poverty, malnutrition and disease across remote communities indicated an acute need for MAF's service.

> ## "
> **Recalling the area from MAF's first survey flight, Stuart stepped out in faith and ordered an additional Cessna 180 aircraft.**

In the late 1950s as MAF was establishing a trusted reputation in Sudan, Africa Inland Mission (AIM) contacted Stuart King to request an air service in East Africa, with operations based out of northern Kenya. Recalling the area from MAF's first survey flight, Stuart stepped out in faith and ordered an additional Cessna 180 aircraft. The Kenyan programme was born in 1959 .

During the early 1980s, MAF accepted the offer of a place in AIM AIR's new hangar, and the two organisations began operating in tandem, sharing a bookings office and a logistics service. During this period, the Kenya programme served surrounding countries such as Burundi, Central African Republic, Comoro Islands, Rwanda, Somalia and Zaire (now the DRC) as permissions allowed.

In recent years, Nairobi has attracted technology and financial service sectors and has seen a boom in infrastructure and increased economic development. But wealth is far from evenly distributed and the needs of isolated people continue to keep MAF's services in high demand. Limited supplies of food, water and healthcare across marginalised border regions are stretched even further to accommodate half a million refugees and MAF flights concentrate mainly on Kenya's northern territories.

MAF's larger Cessna Caravan aircraft offer a weekly shuttle service, which provides smaller NGOs and Church groups with affordable seats on a regular flight path. Overland routes to isolated regions in the northwest involve days of exhausting travel on dilapidated roads, renowned for armed bandits. With MAF, days can be turned into hours or less and the work of aid agencies can be multiplied significantly.

By supporting partners who supply access to clean water and provide emergency food relief, remote communities suffering famine, disease and malnutrition can start to thrive. By flying medical teams with fragile equipment, supplies are not damaged on rough overland journeys and arrive safely and quickly. Vaccines for mothers and children are kept at low temperatures, an impossibility on day-long truck journeys in blistering heat and assisting organisations who offer basic education undoubtedly provides the most effective tool for breaking the cycle of intergenerational poverty.

MAF's services have also helped countless organisations seeking to spread the love and hope of Jesus Christ to some of Kenya's most vulnerable people. Today, MAF's work in Kenya directly supports two AIM Bible translation projects among Rendille and Daasanach tribes, opening the doors to future developments in education, medicine and evangelism. ✚

Main: Kenya, en route to Marsabit

Opposite, top: Waves for Water Country Director Frederick Mango holds a Sawyer water filter kit

COUNTRY STATS

👤 POPULATION
48 million

☆ CAPITAL
Nairobi

💬 LANGUAGES
English, Swahili
+ numerous
indigenous
languages

🚩 ROADS
110,479 miles,
mostly unpaved
(245,000 in the UK)

☀ CLIMATE
Tropical coasts and
arid interior

⩗ LIFE EXPECTANCY
69 years

🚩 MAF AIRSTRIPS
67

🔗 MAF PARTNERS
210 organisations

✚ FLEET
1 x Cessna 206
2 x Cessna 208

ETHIOPIA

KENYA

★ Nairobi

TANZANIA

TIMELINE

○ **1958** Third Cessna 180 aircraft ordered
for Kenya following AIM request
for service

○ **1959** MAF Kenya programme begins

○ **1963** MAF maintenance base established
in Nairobi

○ **1965** First Cessna 206 added to the fleet

○ **1969** MAF's medical safaris begin

○ **1980s** MAF operates from Kenya into
surrounding African countries

○ **1987** Sub-base set up in Kampala, Uganda

○ **1990s** MAF begins providing IT services for
mission agencies

○ **1993** MAF's Sudan operation relocates to
Kenya during civil war

○ **1998** New MAF hangar and Operations
Centre built at Nairobi Airport

○ **2007** Violence erupts in the aftermath of
general elections

○ **2017** Widespread drought devastates
crops across Kenya

> A lot of thanks goes to the MAF
> team for their quickness and
> coordination. We look forward to
> this partnership continuing into
> the future."

Frederick Mango
Kenya Country Director
Waves for Water

Kenya

MAF **Ethiopia** programme
launched

Betty Greene arrives in **Papua,
Indonesia** to help open new
remote airstrips

MAF flies Billy Graham from
Nairobi, Kenya to **Tanzania**;
5,000 come to Christ

MAF **DRC** programme launched

MAF begins work in **Philippines**

First MAF flight in **Tanzania**

MAF **Suriname** programme
launched

MAF forced out of **Sudan**
due to unrest

1960   **1961** **1962** **1963**   **1964**

3

1960, known as the 'Year of Africa' saw a surge of independence movements, with 17 African nations gaining freedom from colonial rule.

These seismic changes presented an opening for MAF to meet acute needs across the continent, with invitations for flight services in Ethiopia, Tanzania, Chad and the DRC.

But with independence came vehement struggles for power and the beginning of a long, bloody chapter marred by conflict and instability across Africa.

The work of MAF and its mission partners was difficult, painstaking and sometimes dangerous, yet God continued to open doors and expand the scope and influence of MAF's flight service.

MAF conducts rescue operations during the **Congo** crisis

Survey of **Chad**

MAF **Chad** programme launched

Second aircraft added to the fleet in **Chad**

MAF **Kalimantan, Indonesia** programme launched

MAF **South Africa** programme launched

1965 **1966** **1967** **1968** **1969**

6000 MILES WITH BILLY GRAHAM

Left: Billy Graham leads prayer before take-off from Nairobi in the three MAF planes, bound for Moshi, Tanzania

Opposite, top: Billy Graham and MAF pilot Ernie Krenzin talk together

Taking Christ literally when He said in the Gospel of Mark, 'Go into all the world and preach the Gospel to all creation' (Mark 16:15), Dr Billy Graham addressed more live audiences than anyone else in history, preaching to over 200 million people across 185 countries and territories.

In 1960, as part of his African Safari for Souls, Billy Graham and his team flew with MAF from Nairobi, Kenya, to Moshi in Tanzania to address 35,000 who gathered at a stadium.

MAF Pilot Gordon Marshall wrote, 'On reaching Moshi, we circled the stadium. It was impressive to see thousands of people, wearing coloured clothing, gathering below. Later, as Billy Graham preached, he looked towards Kilimanjaro: "Your fathers told you that God was in that mountain top," he said. "But God was in Christ reconciling the world unto Himself." '

Over 5,000 stayed to make a commitment to Christ that day.

Billy and his evangelistic team flew a total of 6,000 miles with MAF that year to share the Good News across Africa. MAF counted it a privilege to have played a part in his Safari for Souls, and be used by God to spread the Good News of Christ with thousands of ready hearts. ✦

> "Evangelism has never been tried on such a scale in Africa. God exceeded all expectations in answer to prayer. The people came by the thousands out of jungle, bush and desert to hear the Gospel. Thousands received Christ: The ambassador of Ghana, a member of parliament in Rhodesia, the tribal chief in Nigeria, the senator in Liberia, the Indian Sikh in Kenya, the grandchildren of the Emperor in Ethiopia and thousands more – each with a thrilling story of a transformed life."

Dr Billy Graham
1960

MISSIONARY AVIATION

MAF PLANES AID BILLY GRAHAM

" African Safari for Souls "

6,000 PASSENGER MILES BY MAF

IN

EAST AFRICA

Left : GORDON MARSHALL and HENNIE STEYN, the two MAF pilots from the Sudan, and ERNIE KRENZIN (*right*), the MAF pilot/engineer in East Africa, show Billy Graham, Beverly Shea and Cliff Barrows the air route from NAIROBI in Kenya to MOSHI in Tanganyika.

Gordon Marshall had the distinct privilege of meeting Bishop (then Reverend) Festo Kivengere who was translating for Billy Graham during his Field of Souls tour of East Africa. Gordon also flew Cliff Barrows, Billy's music leader and spoke about how Bishop Festo's story affected his life for the next few decades.

A Bush Pilot's Logbook, **Stephen Marshall and Joyce Sklar-Chik, 2019**

COUNTRY PROFILE:
ETHIOPIA

The Federal Democratic Republic of Ethiopia is a land of natural contrasts. Vast and fertile in the west, numerous rivers and lush, tropical forests are home to the most eclectic bird life in Africa – with more than 856 species recorded to date. But the mountainous north and east have seen some of the hottest temperatures recorded in any inhabited settlement on earth, with average heat in Dallol reaching over 40°C.

As MAF began to operate in Sudan, the 'land of mixed peoples' to the east intrigued MAF's early pioneers for its remoteness, vulnerability and need. In the 1950s, many Ethiopian tribes were still so inaccessible they were completely ungoverned, let alone provided for and their locations were scarcely even known.

The Majang people, for example, had never been accurately located and their language was completely undetermined. Never setting foot outside hidden territories in the rainforest's depths, the Majang suffered many tropical diseases and acute isolation. MAF's mission was to help change this and improve life for the Majang and countless other hidden tribes.

From the earliest stages, medical work and emergencies featured strongly in MAF's Ethiopian air service. In the absence of airstrips, medical supplies were dropped from the air and where planes could touch down, regular bush clinics offered tribespeople their first access to medical help.

> ## "
> **Airstrips in Ethiopia are unique, hazardous and hugely varied. Some have curves and bends; some slope sideways, some have optical illusions and others drop away with alarming abruptness.**

MAF operated in Ethiopia for almost 40 years but a halt to operations in Ethiopia during the turbulent 1970s and 1980s was a desperately difficult time. MAF helped from outside to reach those crippled by Africa's worst-seen famine which affected around eight million people in the early 1980s.

Airstrips in Ethiopia are unique, hazardous and hugely varied. Some have curves and bends; some slope sideways, some have optical illusions and others drop away with alarming abruptness. Each demanded every ounce of experience, skill and faith from MAF pilots. But although often short, every MAF flight in Ethiopia saved days of slow, difficult and expensive overland travel and helped alleviate suffering, facilitate growth and spread the Gospel message.

In 1998 MAF was refused the permissions required to continue operating and the door to Ethiopia closed. A private air charter company named Abyssinian Flight Services (AFS) continues to operate in Ethiopia, initially leasing then eventually purchasing an MAF Cessna Caravan aircraft to respond to the Ethiopian drought of 1999. Today, AFS operates 12 Cessna aircraft, 4 Diamond aircraft and runs a private pilot training academy. ✚

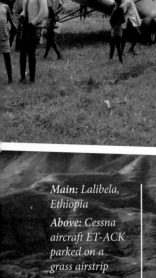

Main: Lalibela, Ethiopia

Above: Cessna aircraft ET-ACK parked on a grass airstrip

Right: Tom Frank, MAF Ethiopia Pilot, after being awarded RAF wings, 1958

COUNTRY STATS

👤 **POPULATION**
109 million

☆ **CAPITAL**
Addis Ababa

💬 **LANGUAGES**
Amharic, Oromo
+ indigenous
languages

🚩 **ROADS**
74,670 miles,
mostly unpaved
(245,000 in the UK)

☀ **CLIMATE**
Tropical monsoon

〰 **LIFE EXPECTANCY**
63 years

MAF NEWS

In 1984, a Twin Otter, owned by World Vision and flown by MAF pilot Keith Ketchum, had been flying famine relief into Ethiopia around the clock. Keith flew the BBC team who broadcast first-seen footage of dying babies and fly-covered corpses, which sparked a world-wide awakening.

Overnight, money began pouring in at an unprecedented rate to help those who were starving to death. As the UN warned 150 million people faced starvation across Africa, Bob Geldof launched Live Aid, filling Wembley stadium in London and John F Kennedy Stadium in Pennsylvania to reach a global audience of 1.9 billion – 40% of the world's population.

By 2000, MAF pilots had flown Bob Geldof and the BBC 19 times.

> It's quite sobering to look back on the week and reflect on how many missionaries have come to depend on MAF. I think of what delays could mean and the large number of people who'd be affected. The ramifications are endless. It's wonderful to know that the same God who has given us this job is in control of all circumstances!"

Tom Frank
MAF Ethiopia Pilot

COUNTRY TIMELINE

1960 Pilot Bob Hutchins agrees to fly for MAF in Ethiopia, based in Jimma

1961 Aircraft bought by UK supporters, sadly damaged in early landing

1963 Three pilots facilitate a second aircraft and expand operation

1974 Six aircraft in operation

1977 Marxist government restrictions forces MAF operations to cease

1977 Somalian invasion, Ogaden War begins

1983 - '85 Famine affects 8 million, at least 1 million die; Live Aid is launched

1990 Soviet Union terminates aid agreements

1992 MAF operations restart and rapidly expand

1995 Ethiopia holds first multiparty elections

1998 MAF refused permission to continue flying, programme closes

1999 MAF helps establish Abyssinian Flight Services (AFS), leasing an aircraft for rural flight charters, overseen by former MAF Pilot Solomon Gizaw

2000 MAF maintains a strategic partnership with AFS, ensuring access to remote areas

REACHING THE MAJANG

Harvey and Lavina Hoekstra had been working with a people the Ethiopian government called Mesengo, but the people themselves called their tribe *Majang*. Stuart King recalls:

The Majang live in a place named Godare, deep in the dense rainforests of south-west Ethiopia. MAF had carried out an aerial survey to chart their location. Trekking for seven days through unknown forest to reach them, Harvey and Lavina finally arrived with their three-year-old son Paul to set up a new home.

MAF was their only way of receiving supplies and all the earthly possessions they couldn't drag through the jungle.

As the Cessna 185 aircraft flew low over the dense treetops, I fixed a rope to one of the cargo tie-down rings and secured it round my waist. Wind was blasting in where the right-hand door had once been with a steady roar.

'Now!' shouted Gordon Marshall from the cockpit.

I pushed a sack out and watched it tumble towards the ground. Gordon opened the throttle and started climbing, then banked as we circled and came round over the clearing again. I pushed another sack out, very thankful for the rope around my waist. Below I had a fleeting glimpse of Harvey in his familiar khaki shorts and white pith helmet. Some forest dwellers were standing with him, looking up and waving.

In three months, we made 40 drops for the Hoekstra family, delivering food, medical supplies, tools and building materials. It was an exciting

"It took us several hours to get carriers organised and six mules loaded. Even at best the trail was barely passable. Vines, thorns and brush, fallen trees and 10 or 11 river crossings all slowed us down. Once I turned my head to see Paul pulled backwards off his horse with a vine wrapped around his neck. He had a bandage around him the rest of the journey.

"Once in Majang country, we found local chiefs were helpful and rounded up whole families with men, women and even children each carrying something. We slept that night in wet bedrolls with a single mosquito net stretched over our three heads. We were glad when daylight broke.

"The next morning, Balte, the local Chief turned up with about 30 men to build 2 glorified Majang shacks for us. Those first days brought scores of Majang out of the forest to see these strange white people. They moved right in with us, coming in through the door and even window openings. They stayed and watched everything we did.

Harvey Hoekstra's account of their journey to meet the Majang

flying challenge for us MAF crew. For Harvey, Lavina and Paul, it was a lifeline.

As trust was built, Harvey paid a large number of tribesmen to clear an airstrip, to allow us to land. A group of Majang gathered with Harvey to greet us as we jumped from the aircraft; chattering black and white colobus monkeys scrambling up and down trees that were 130 feet tall. We studied the people with interest. They were handsome, with smiling faces, wearing loincloths, leaves or occasionally shorts, with coloured beads round their necks, arms and waists.

Some carried spears, others had ancient rifles brought from distant trading posts. Some of them held little musical instruments which they plucked to produce a curious musical tune.

Over time, MAF helped fly in prefabricated sections, carefully designed to fit into the small MAF Cessna aircraft, to form a workshop. Then, a clinic, a schoolroom and a house for the Hoekstra family sprang up underneath the giant trees. A year later, 100 Majang met regularly to worship God.

The Majang chose five strategic places where they hoped to establish new congregations of believers and sent two of their number to each. What God had been leading the Hoekstra family to do, He was now leading the Majang to do as well.

Almost daily, Majang took out sturdy little hand-turned cassette players with taped messages prepared by Harvey telling of freedom in the love of Christ. One group commented, 'Why have we never heard this Word before?'

Many were baptised and work continues today in the Majang community.

In 2011, I heard from Denny Hoekstra – Harvey's eldest son who became an MAF Pilot and Programme Manager in Ethiopia. Finally the Majang had the Word of God in their own language. ✠

Opposite, top: Two of the Majang women

Bottom: The Cessna 185 in a jungle clearing

This page, l-r: Dropping supplies from the air. A Cessna 185. Unloading the plane at Godare

COUNTRY PROFILE:
THE DEMOCRATIC REPUBLIC OF THE CONGO

The Democratic Republic of the Congo (DRC) is the second-largest country in Africa by size, and the fourth largest by population. Formerly named Zaïre under the presidency of Mobutu Sese Seko, who stayed in power for 32 years until 1997, the country was dragged through a long season of ethnic violence and brutal civil war.

MAF was invited to begin operating in the early 1960s in Kinshasa, western DRC, following the turbulent period of independence from Belgium, when many Christian missionaries were killed or held hostage. Embassies declared that a more dependable air service was required if missionaries were to stay in the country and carry out humanitarian work.

In 1966, the first MAF family moved to Bunia, eastern DRC, where MAF's operations began. In 1967, the family moved to Nyankunde in the north-east to partner with *Centre Médical Evangélique* (CME), a newly established evangelical medical trust covering the area.

For 30 years, MAF provided a flying doctor service, medical supply line and HF radio communication network to rural clinics and hospitals across the country. Many missionaries were able to stay in the DRC because of MAF's trusted service.

In 1996, the First Congo War resulted in widespread evacuations throughout eastern DRC. Most MAF families were reassigned to different programmes. One MAF base was looted and the others were closed. The situation finally escalated when Rwanda invaded, soon joined by Uganda, Burundi, Angola, Sudan and Eritrea. Hundreds of thousands lost their lives.

No sooner had MAF slowly started to relaunch operations, when the Second Congo War erupted in 1998, resulting in more evacuations and the decision for many mission groups not to return. MAF operations were run from Kampala, Uganda and flight permissions were suspended.

Over the years, MAF has served across the entire vast country. In 2001, one MAF family moved back to Nyankunde, only to have their home ransacked in 2002 and many of their possessions looted. The entire MAF base was destroyed and many houses across the town were torn apart. It was a terrifying ordeal and thousands of people lost their lives.

When war finally came to an end in 2003, 5.4 million lives had been lost. Today more than 100 rebel groups continue to operate in eastern DRC and the security situation remains far from stable.

Yet, in response to high demand and God's leading, MAF's operation began to expand again so that healing, reconciliation and community development could touch a nation that has been devastated for decades.

During the Ebola outbreaks in 2014 and 2018, MAF was on standby to offer emergency evacuation flights, deliver blood samples and fly those working to combat the virus. Once an experimental vaccine became available in 2018, thousands of doses were distributed. Key personnel were transported quickly and safely. One of the passengers was the most Reverend Justin Welby, Archbishop of Canterbury, who visited two Ebola treatment sites in October 2019 to speak hope to those trying to rebuild their lives.

Continuing to provide emergency medical evacuations, transport medicine and facilitate an interdenominational Christian movement, in recent years MAF's service has become a lifeline for hundreds of communities and missionaries across the DRC. ✢

COUNTRY STATS

- 👤 **POPULATION**
  85.3 million

- ☆ **CAPITAL**
  Kinshasa

- 💬 **LANGUAGES**
  French, Lingala, Kingwana

- ☀ **CLIMATE**
  Tropical; hot and humid

- 〰 **LIFE EXPECTANCY**
  58.1 years

- 🚩 **ROADS**
  152,373 miles, mostly unpaved (245,000 in the UK)

- 🚩 **MAF AIRSTRIPS**
  180

- 🔗 **MAF PARTNERS**
  100 organisations

- ✛ **FLEET**
  2 x Cessna 206
  4 x Cessna 208
  1 x Pilatus PC-12

D.R.C.
★ Kinshasa

MAF NEWS

In 2002, tribal war exploded into Nyankunde where pilot David Jacobsson and his family were based. While Dave was flying to pick up a medical team, Donna remained at home with their two sons, 9-year-old Matthew and 22-month Andrew. Armed men forced their way into the house, it was a terrifying ordeal.

Donna recalls: 'It got hot very quickly, suddenly there was gunfire and within minutes Nyankunde was surrounded. We met in the living room to pray before the children hid under a bed.

'The first group kicked the door in, and a dozen soldiers were outside. The dog was barking. I spoke to them with the utmost respect. They wanted money and our radio, which they took immediately – it was screwed into the shelf so they took the whole thing.

'They took all the money we owned – God reminded me of our education fund and a hospitality gift which I had buried in my drawer. It's as if He provided that cash for our moment of need. They allowed me to transmit a final radio message – I prayed it would reach Dave.

'We lost many friends and neighbours. It was very difficult. The boys and I were evacuated to Kenya, but the massacre continued for ten days. God has done such an amazing miracle in healing me over the years. I look back and know the Lord was definitely with me.'

TIMELINE

- **1960** Independence from Belgium
- **1961** MAF arrives in western DRC to support *Operation Doctor* in Kinshasa
- **1966** MAF arrives in eastern DRC, partnering with CME hospital in Nyankunde
- **1981** Bukavu base opens serving Kivu and Maniema regions in the east
- **1984** Nebobongo base opens to serve the church and hospital in the north
- **1996** First Congo War, all MAF bases except Kinshasa evacuated
- **1998** Second Congo War, many more missions evacuated
- **1999** MAF operations resume
- **2002** MAF staff escape Nyankunde massacre, operations relocate to Kampala, Uganda
- **2006** First democratic elections take place
- **2007** MAF operations begin in Bunia, MAF responds to Ebola outbreak in the west
- **2010** MAF base reopened at Lubumbashi, southern DRC
- **2014** MAF responds to the Ebola crisis
- **2019** MAF flies Archbishop Justin Welby to visit Ebola victims

Democratic Republic of the Congo

THE FLEET:
CESSNA U206 STATIONAIR

For many years, the Cessna U206 Stationair was the mainstay of MAF's fleet, proving itself to be a very adaptable aircraft for mission flying.

First flown in 1964, the piston-engined C206 can carry five passengers, or up to 816kg of cargo. It is still in production today, in a much-modernised format.

Most of MAF's C206s are actually U206s – the U stands for 'Utility', indicating that the aircraft has a range of factory modifications to make it more suitable for carrying cargo as well as passengers. The most significant of these modifications is a large, double door in the side of the fuselage, making it easier to load bulky items into the aircraft.

MAF's C206s are also upgraded to make them better suited to bush-flying: the wheels and brakes are upgraded, with larger diameter tyres fitted; a V-shaped brace is installed in the windscreen area, to strengthen the cabin framework; and radios and other avionics are improved, to make navigation safer and easier.

One strength of the C206 is the ability to get in and out of shorter airstrips compared to the larger, faster Cessna 208 Caravan aircraft.

The main drawback of the C206 is its piston engine. Because it burns increasingly scarce and expensive Avgas, the C206 is not as cost-effective per passenger mile as other, turbine-powered aircraft in MAF's fleet. For this reason, the number of C206s operated by MAF has been reducing in recent years – a trend that is likely to continue. ✈

Main: 5Y-PTL at sunset in LogLogo, Kenya

Main: Lalibela, Ethiopia

GENERAL CHARACTERISTICS

Crew
one

Capacity
five passengers

Length
8.61m (28ft 3in)

Wingspan
10.97m (36ft)

Height
2.83m (9ft 3½in)

Wing area
16.30m² (175½sq. ft)

Empty weight
987kg (2,176lb)

Max. take off weight
1,633kg (3,600lb)

Powerplant
one Lycoming IO-540-AC1A naturally-aspirated air-cooled flat-six (220kW/300hp)

Propeller
three-bladed McCauley metal constant-speed

PERFORMANCE

Max. speed
151kn (280km/h, 174mph) at sea level

Cruise speed
142kn (262km/h, 163mph) at 6,200ft, 75% power

Stall speed
55kn (101km/h, 63mph) flaps down

Range
730nmi (1,350km, 840mi)

Service ceiling
15,700ft

Rate of climb
988ft/min

WHAT THE PILOT SAYS

'With our five-passenger Cessna 206, we can economically transport missionaries, a medevac patient, or around 400kgs of desperately needed supplies or vaccines to very remote jungle communities.'

Nick Frey
Nick Frey, MAF pilot DRC

COUNTRY PROFILE:
CHAD

The Republic of Chad is Africa's largest landlocked nation, almost nine times the size of the United Kingdom. Known as the 'Desert Heart of Africa', the inhospitable north is covered by vast, empty miles of Sahara Desert. Inhabited only by a scattering of nomadic Muslim herdsmen, very little else exists in this barren landscape. Transport is limited to narrow tracks and many still use draft animals to travel across the sand. Landmines continue to present danger to anyone daring enough to wander across the endless desert.

To the south, subsistence farmers struggle to survive in very hot, humid swamplands and Chad is still among the bottom three of the least-developed countries in the world. Lake Chad, once one of Africa's largest wetlands, has seen dramatic decline in recent years. Climate change, overuse of water and widespread deforestation have reduced its size by 95% since the 1970s, hitting fishermen, wildlife and communities with increasing hunger and poverty.

The stark contrasts between north and south present a fragile security situation, preventing foreign investment which could develop the significant deposits of uranium, gold, bauxite and oil.

MAF was invited into Chad in 1965, initially to support Christian nurses, doctors and evangelists living in lonely missional communities along Lake Chad's shoreline. Before MAF's amphibious aircraft arrived, travellers covered miles of dangerous shifting sand and swamp to bring medical supplies and encouragement to those living in extreme poverty.

After a survey flight in 1965, MAF launched its operation the following year with a Cessna 185 amphibious aircraft. A dedication service was planned at a quiet spot on the banks of Lake Chad with a handful of local missionaries. Somehow, word had spread and at least 7,000 people turned out for the occasion. The enthusiasm for MAF's service was overwhelming.

Throughout the decade that followed, the atmosphere in Chad became more and more hostile, with political unrest and persecution of the Church spreading throughout the country. MAF was finally forced to leave in 1979 when civil war broke out in the capital N'Djamena.

Despite this, only two years later, permissions were granted for MAF to return, and medical and evangelistic work expanded from Bébalém. From there MAF conducted a widespread famine-relief operation, calling on 18 ex-MAF relief pilots and aircraft maintenance engineers to respond to the humanitarian emergency.

Ever since relaunching the programme, Chad has endured constant tension between rebel groups in the north and south. MAF staff have become accustomed to evacuations and operations are regularly suspended.

Today, MAF's presence in Chad is just as vital as it has ever been. Our partners rely on MAF's dependable service to meet the needs of the most vulnerable communities, knowing that an evacuation is possible in the face of unrest, persecution or medical emergency.

MAF flights provide relief organisations with essential access to the country's remotest regions, supporting water and medical projects, Bible translation work and life-changing development initiatives. ✈

> **❝**
> **MAF was invited into Chad in 1965, initially to support Christian nurses, doctors and evangelists.**

Main: Sahara Desert, Chad

Above: A medical safari flight in Chad saves precious time and allows the doctor to visit numerous communities within the space of a week or 10 days

COUNTRY STATS

👤 **POPULATION**
15.8 million

☆ **CAPITAL**
N'Djamena

💬 **LANGUAGES**
French, Arabic, Sara
+ more than 120
local dialects

🚩 **ROADS**
24,854 miles –
mostly unpaved
(245,000 in the UK)

☀ **CLIMATE**
Tropical in south,
desert in north

〰 **LIFE EXPECTANCY**
57.5 years

🚩 **MAF AIRSTRIPS**
29

🔗 **MAF PARTNERS**
36 organisations

✈ **FLEET**
1 x Cessna 182 SMA
1 x Cessna 208

LIBYA

NIGER

CHAD

SUDAN

⭐ N'Djamena

C.A.R.

That evening, as we were having supper, there was a knock on the door. Two of the elders came in. 'They say they have a gift for the men with the aeroplane,' the missionary translated. 'They heard you want to bring an aeroplane to Chad. They want to be the first to give something towards buying a plane to work in their country. They believe it could help their people and spread the Good News of God.'

We were staggered. Here was a church in one of the poorest countries in Africa, whose people lived barely at subsistence level. Yet out of their poverty they wanted to help buy an aeroplane. God had put His seal upon Chad.

Extract from *Hope Has Wings*, Stuart King, 2004, pp215-216

 MAF is a huge help in our logistics, facilitating what we are doing; whether it's getting us, or people we invite, across the country, transporting material or even mail."

Association for Development and Peace

TIMELINE

- **1960** Independance from France
- **1965** Survey by Stuart King and John Ducker in Cessna 206 aircraft
- **1966** Chad operation launched at Fort-Lamy
- **1968** MAF base opened at Koumra; a second C206 aircraft added to the fleet
- **1973** Violent practices under President Tombalbaye and persecution of Christians
- **1975** MAF Pilot Claude Jacot sadly dies of hepatitis after six months' service
- **1979** Civil war prevents MAF operations; aircraft and staff relocate to other programmes
- **1981** MAF Programme reopens in Bébalém
- **1985** Widespread famine, MAF launches emergency response
- **2005** New hangar and offices built at N'Djamena
- **2010** MAF officially registered as an independent NGO in Chad
- **2012** Cessna 182 SMA joins the fleet
- **2016** MAF granted Aircraft Maintenance Organisation approval

Chad

AIRSTRIP OPENING:
THE CANOE FROM THE SKY

Above: Betty Greene

Right: Betty Greene (L) and Leona St. John, embark on a trek to Hitadipa, Dutch New Guinea, April 1962

Opposite: Betty with missionary Bill Cutts and Leona St. John. Celebrations after the first flight into Hitadipa

In November 1960, Betty Greene heard about a new airstrip that was to be opened in the remote village of Hitadipa among the Moni people of central Papua, Indonesia.

The new opening would save missionary couple Bill and Grace Cutts a three-day trek to reach the next town and offer a new way of life for the isolated community.

But this three-day trek must first be made by Betty herself.

As the Cessna aircraft circled around Pogapa – a nine hundred foot long rocky ledge six thousand feet up a mountain – Betty understood why it was the most difficult landing in the country – perhaps even the world.

With no one to run and hold an old white sheet to form a windsock, Pilot George Boggs studied the trees for some idea of wind direction.

Expertly touching down short

of the sheer drop into a canyon at the edge of the runway, George killed the engine and Betty hopped out. 'Well Betty, I guess you're on your own,' he said before saying a short prayer and leaving her with a group of indigenous guides and local missionary Leona St John.

Betty studied the group of men, dressed only with a string around their waist. Three carried equipment and food, which rested on their backs, held in place by a strap from the forehead. As the reverberations of the departing Cessna's engine faded, the sense of isolation washed over her. Anything could happen in the next three days.

The highland jungle was trapped in a constant state of bloody upheaval, with neighbouring tribes blaming evil curses for illness and responding with violent acts of murderous retaliation. If a man was killed, his wife would be martyred so she could lay beside him on

death platforms suspended high in the treetops. The birds would peck them to the bone as they entered into the afterlife.

Bill and Grace were here to show the Moni that there was another way to live.

As the group trekked deep into the jungle, they were faced with a fragile bridge of woven vines suspended 20 feet above a furiously swirling river. Betty could feel cold sweat beading on her forehead and the first taste of debilitating fear. Aided by her Moni guide, she slowly edged inch by inch to the other side.

'Last month Grace was sick,' said Leona as Betty's pulse slowed to normal. 'Can you imagine crossing that bridge with a high fever and dizziness?' Betty shook her head. Each aching muscle and terrifying vine bridge became suddenly worthwhile as their adventure intensified.

After two days, the group encountered villagers on one mountain ridge who spoke to Leona in their unfathomable dialect. Concerned, Leona turned back to Betty and immediately she knew something was wrong.

'War,' said Leona sadly. 'Fighting, two villages ahead. But there is no other route – we must pray we don't get caught up in it.'

Every cracking twig or muffled sound was investigated for fear of ambush. Betty could

hear her heart thudding, praying it wouldn't give them away.

Slowly emerging at the next village, the group faced the sickening sight of burned huts, looted storehouses and dead bodies. Leona explained that this village would endure more agony in the weeks to come, as the Moni believed that a good show of grief would help the departed arrive at their next life.

'They might return to claim the fingers of children to be sure plenty of wailing and weeping will rise up the mountain,' Leona added, sadly.

Betty's stomach churned.

These people needed to hear the Gospel and experience its freedom. Her little plane had never felt so valuable.

As the group walked down the final mountain ridge, Betty heard strains of tuneful hymns – the sweet singing had never sounded so welcoming. Adrenaline and relief rushed through her veins.

Proudly welcoming them into his tiny home, yet to be filled with earthly possessions, Bill Cutts showed Betty the work he and the local men had achieved on the airstrip. It was in perfect condition and Betty radioed George with the good news that he could make his first landing.

By 10:30am, a crowd of Moni had gathered, singing and shouting Bible verses they had memorised.

Soon, the Cessna 180 aircraft was circling overhead and the group broke into wild cheering and dancing. The atmosphere was electric with joy, victory and pride.

As the plane rolled to a stop, the crowd surged towards the 'canoe from the sky' to talk to the man who had been 'carried in its belly'. Many hours of feasting and dancing followed.

That day changed history for the Hitadipa and was one Betty would never, ever forget. ✛

LOCATION PROFILE:
KALIMANTAN

Located to the south of the island of Borneo, the Indonesian province of Kalimantan is covered by inhospitable jungles, raging rivers and dangerous swamps, which prevent land travel for the vast number of indigenous tribes scattered across tiny, isolated villages.

Its name is derived from the ancient word *Kalamanthana*, which means 'burning weather'; thus warning of its hot and humid tropical climate. An active volcano and seasonal wildfires, causing poor air quality, ravage the already scorching habitat, putting many lives in danger.

Poverty, unemployment and inadequate infrastructure prevent development and progress for the people of Kalimantan.

Beginning a flight service in the east of the island, MAF's early ministry focused primarily on serving Indonesian nationals working to help those facing poverty and isolation. Passengers in the early 1970s included Western missionaries connected to a small network of Bible schools, who sought to spread the Gospel and translate the Bible into local languages.

As Kalimantan's indigenous Church emerged and began to grow, MAF was instrumental in serving pastors and evangelists, helping them spread the Gospel to remote villages otherwise inaccessible by road. Helping establish a radio communication system across the province, MAF enabled churches to connect and deepen their support for one another and fledgling Christian communities began

> ## "
> **Today, MAF's aircraft provide regular, dependable flights for partners distributing lifechanging cargo**

to thrive. The radio network became so popular it was extended to many other NGOs working across Kalimantan.

A floatplane base was established in the mid-1990s at Palangkaraya to assist a medical clinic run by Wycliffe Bible Translators and life-saving healthcare began to reach those living along four major river systems. As medicine became available, so did Christian education materials and the Gospel message spread along the waterways.

Today, MAF's aircraft provide regular, dependable flights for partners distributing lifechanging cargo and evacuating critical patients to hospital. An MAF-run guesthouse for relatives of medevac'd patients at the hospital in Tarakan is deeply appreciated by those who would otherwise stay separated from loved ones in their critical stages of recovery.

Thanks to MAF's service in Kalimantan, life in remote villages is constantly improving due to better living conditions. Educational needs are being met because teachers, students and resources can be flown in. Health is improving through vaccinations, personnel and those working to provide clean water systems, all flown in by MAF. And many more people are hearing the Gospel thanks to the growth and support of the Church. ✢

Above: 'Robyn's Rock', after Robyn Pratt, the wife of former MAF pilot Jason Pratt

Right: An airstrip at Kalimantan

Opposite, top to bottom: Children at the floatplane dock; Pastor flights in Kalimantan

LOCATION STATS

👤 **POPULATION**
15.8 million

⭐ **CAPITAL**
Jakarta

💬 **LANGUAGES**
Bahasa Indonesia, English, Dutch, Javanese

〰 **LIFE EXPECTANCY**
73.2 years

☀ **CLIMATE**
Tropical; hot, humid

🚩 **ROADS**
308,000 miles, some unpaved (245,000 in the UK)

🏴 **MAF AIRSTRIPS**
16

🔗 **MAF PARTNERS**
7 organisations

✛ **FLEET**
2 x Cessna 206
2 x Quest Kodiak 100

MALAYSIA

Tarakan

KALIMANTAN
Indonesia

⭐ **Jakarta**

TIMELINE

○ **1969** MAF programme launched in Tarakan

○ **1995** Floatplane base opened at Palangkaraya

○ **2004** MAF facility at Palangkarya destroyed by fire, aircraft are not damaged but grounded

○ **2013** MAF opens a hospital guest house in Tarakan

○ **2018** MAF responds to a 7.5 magnitude earthquake which hits the Central Sulawesi province

❝ MAF has been a big part of building the Church in Kalimantan from years ago until now. In many places, MAF is still very much needed."

Yusmanto Luis
Pastor

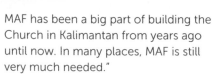

Kalimantan

CESSNA 185 SKYWAGON

Like many of Cessna's designs, the 185 Skywagon was an iterative development of an earlier model – in this case the venerable Cessna 180.

Effectively a strengthened and more powerful C180 and often described as an 'aerial pickup truck', the C185 would become a mainstay of MAF operations across the world. Serving either as conventional bush aircraft or as floatplanes, the C185s represented a great advance in carrying capacity over the older C180s, with a 'useful load' increase of up to 270kg.

Possibly the most well-known of MAF's C185s was PK-MCB – nicknamed 'Charlie Brown' – which served the people of Kalimantan, in the Republic of Indonesia for almost 50 years. Deployed to the island of Borneo in 1969, PK-MCB was initially operated as a conventional land-based aircraft, until its conversion into a floatplane during the 1990s. In this role, the aircraft provided a vital lifeline to waterside communities throughout Kalimantan, until its retirement from service with MAF in 2017. However, this wasn't the end of the story for Charlie Brown! PK-MCB now has a starring role as the centrepiece of a display, promoting the work of MAF, at the Verkehrshaus transport museum in Lucerne, Switzerland.

"

The newer design proved extremely effective and offered great advantages in terms of pilot visibility and handling on the ground.

Right: Cessna 185 Skywagon from Stuart King's album

Opposite: A medevac in Kalimantan. Locals carry a little girl to the plane

FACTFILE

GENERAL CHARACTERISTICS

Crew
one

Capacity
five passengers

Length
7.85m (25ft 9in)

Wingspan
10.92m (35ft 10in)

Height
2.36m (7ft 9in)

Wing area
16.2m² (174sq. ft)

Empty weight
793kg (1,748lb)

Gross weight
1,520kg (3,350lb)

Powerplant
one Continental IO-520-D, (220kW/300hp)

Propeller
two- or three-bladed constant-speed

PERFORMANCE

Max. speed
148kn (274km/h, 170mph)

Cruise speed
145kn (269km/h, 167mph)

Stall speed
49kn (91km/h, 56mph)

Range
720nmi (1,330km, 830mi)

Service ceiling
17,150ft

Rate of climb
1,010ft/min

Although still highly effective, most of MAF's C185s were progressively replaced in the 1980s and 1990s by more modern Cessna aircraft, such as the C206 and C210. These later models featured 'tricycle' undercarriages with a nosewheel, rather than the dated 'taildragger' design of the C180. Despite reservations about how this wheel arrangement would cope with the unprepared airstrips served by MAF, the newer design proved extremely effective and offered great advantages in terms of pilot visibility and handling while on the ground. According to Stuart King, the C206 also had 'appreciably more cabin space than the C185... and was better suited to carry stretcher cases or freight'. ✈

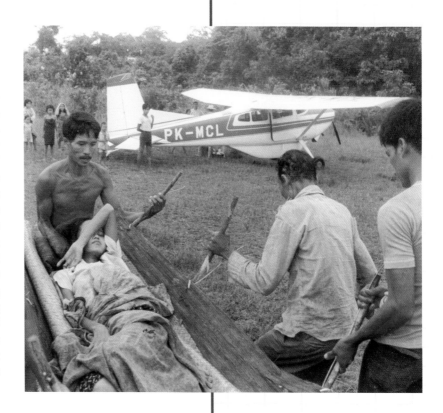

MAF begins a programme in **Colombia**

MAF launches a programme in **Nicaragua**

MAF **Arnhem Land** programme launched in the Northern Territory of **Australia**

MAF **Canada** is founded

Six aircraft operating in **Ethiopia**, including MAF's Cessna 210, ideal for long distances

MAF survey of **Tanzania**

MAF **Finland** formed

1970 1971 1972 1973 1974 1975 1976

4

THE 1970s

As MAF entered its third decade in Africa, enormous changes were evident in the less-developed areas where MAF worked.

The emergence of new independent nations meant MAF served against a background of unrest and uncertainty. As the need for aviation increased, MAF's aircraft became more sophisticated and training developed to meet growing demand and increasing challenges.

There had also been tremendous growth of the African Church, with MAF aircraft essential for local pastors to reach isolated areas, opening villages up to long-term physical and spiritual help. As word about MAF spread, offices began to open across Europe to help raise awareness, support and assist skilled missionaries joining the expanding mission.

MAF conducts relief flights following a severe earthquake in **Papua, Indonesia**

MAF **Tanzania** programme launched

Government restrictions force MAF operations to cease in **Ethiopia**

MAF's hovercraft project launched in Lake Chad, west-central **Africa**

MAF begins flight operations in **Guatemala**

MAF **Netherlands** formed

Civil war forces MAF operations to cease in **Chad**

MAF operations reopen in **Sudan**

1977   **1978** **1979**

AIRSTRIP OPENING:
BALA AT LAST

MAF Pilots Paul Balisky and Bob Hedderly describe the opening of a new airstrip in Ethiopia, 1971.

Following our first abortive attempt to reach and check the new airstrip at Bala, Ethiopia, we set off again in early October. The rainy season was almost over, but the trail was liberally spread with deep mud holes. It would be a two-day mule ride.

We set off in good weather, but by mid-afternoon, we plodded slowly through a terrific thunderstorm. The mules carefully picked their way through swirling water often nine inches deep.

When we finally arrived at Bala at nightfall, it was to find people very discouraged. 'We did all the work and you didn't come,' they said. 'The witchdoctor said a plane would never land here.'

Apologising for the delay, we congratulated them on their hard work and explained the plane was expected on Saturday at 10:30am. We spent the next day carefully checking the strip, making corner markers and an 'aiming spot' for the plane's arrival.

'Please forgive us for not believing you,' they said, as we were offered a feast in anticipation of MAF's long-awaited first landing.

By ten o'clock, about 400 people had arrived. Ten minutes later, we heard and then saw the plane to the west, passing out of sight as Pilot Verne Sikkema looked for the new strip. Faces fell until two or three minutes later, the aircraft reappeared and headed straight for us. A careful inspection, steady approach, smooth touchdown, splutter from the engine and the plane was stationary amid a sea of

Above: Joyce and Bob Hedderly

Right and Opposite: MAF in rural Ethiopia

inquisitive faces.

The landing brought many others hurrying to the airstrip, where they found Paul and Verne perched on the wings of the plane speaking through an interpreter to the crowd, now almost 1,000 strong.

Verne explained the use and dangers of the plane and expressed MAF's desire to help them medically, with education and to know the Living God. Paul then simply told the Gospel story – what a pulpit!

It was great to leave the mule and return swiftly to Jimma, praying that the Lord would pour out His Spirit upon these people. ✈

A NIGHT AT NAKURIO

MAF Pilot Les Brown gives a first-hand account of a medical outreach in northern Kenya, 1971.

We took off from Kalokol, Kenya in our Cessna 207 aircraft about mid-afternoon, heading south down the western shore of Lake Rudolph. AIM doctor Dick Anderson was on board with local pastor, Peter and we carried 300 pounds of food for the schoolchildren and teachers at Nakurio. The 20-minute flight would have taken the best part of a day by Land Rover.

Below us the airstrip was extremely difficult to see, however we just made out the piles of bleached bones which acted as runway markers.

Dr Anderson set up a clinic in the little grass-roofed school building, using a small folding table we had brought along. It was the only piece of furniture, apart from several small tree trunks making seats for the children. Soon a crowd gathered, so we moved outside for a small evangelistic meeting, with hymns in the local language and a short message. Pastor Peter continued to preach while Dr Anderson returned to his patients.

Then, a couple of young warriors appeared on the scene, spears in hand. These were Epiot's sons, inviting us to their village for the evening – three miles away.

Epiot, an ex-chief and wise man, has more wives than you or I have children. Admitted twice to the mission hospital, he has become a good friend of Dr Anderson. Having heard the plane overhead, Epiot immediately despatched his sons to meet us.

Above and opposite page:
Dr Dick Anderson at Nakurio

Right: *MAF Cessna 207 at Nakurio*

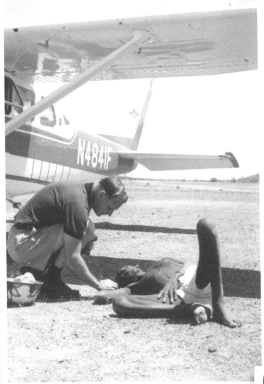

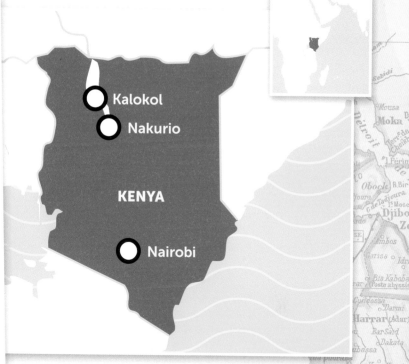

Just before dark, we set off on the three-mile trek. It was a wonder our guides could find their way in the featureless countryside. As we approached the village, I could see Epiot kneeling on his skin mat by the light of a fire, his wives sitting in the soft sand around him.

Giving a warm greeting in his jovial way, a wife was sent to fetch an old wooden chair and an empty box for us to sit on. Sitting at Epiot's right hand, a middle-aged son produced a gourd of dried meat which he offered around like a box of chocolates. I was given a mug of tea – very acceptable after our long walk.

After a while, Dr Anderson asked Epiot if he could speak to the people. Wives and children were sent to call their neighbours and soon a little crowd gathered under the starry sky. They loved learning hymns in their language and were very responsive to the Word of God.

It was a wonder we found our way back with no moon. In the absence of mosquitos, we slept under the stars. At sunrise, we found Epiot's gift, a big, fat sheep, standing against the thatched wall of the school, waiting to be persuaded into the back of the plane. ✛

A BEAUTIFUL MOMENT

In 1973, a young boy living in Degan, a small village in northern Ethiopia, opened his eyes to a murmur of voices. Barely awake, he sensed concern in his parents' voices. He was sick. Very sick.

Opening them again, this time to a blur of faces, he picked out members of their mission community, heads bowed. They gathered around his bed to pray.

Andrew Cunningham was born in Ethiopia to a British father and Swiss mother, both serving with Echoes of Service, a Brethren mission reaching villages with medicine and the love of Christ. United in their training as nurses Andrew's parents were destined for mission life from the beginning.

But today, the physical condition of their six-year-old son was out of their hands. Malaria was taking hold and Andrew wouldn't survive a day's overland travel to the capital, Addis Ababa.

'I wonder if we could get in touch with MAF?' someone said. A radio call was made. The family waited. Andrew closed his eyes.

'I was in and out of consciousness,' recalls Andrew. 'But I remember feeling a change of atmosphere in that room. It was a sense of relief and hope.

An MAF plane was flying south *en route* to the capital, and could land at Kombolcha, 15 miles away. There were two spare seats; it was a lifeline.

A little while later, Andrew and his mother made their way to Kombolcha. 'I remember waiting in a small shack,' reflects Andrew. 'I suppose it was the terminal. I saw the plane at the end of the airstrip, but I was desperately ill – I could barely take it all in.'

Landing in Addis Ababa Andrew received medical attention from a doctor who was able to give him the lifesaving medication he needed to make a full recovery. 'It wasn't until weeks, months and even years later that I have realised the gravity of that flight,' he says. 'Those two spare seats – they were provided by God. It was His hand on my life. Even now, it makes me realise how precious every single life is.'

The family stayed in Ethiopia as missionaries until 1978, when they were forced to leave under the communist government. Andrew maintained a loose connection with MAF and became an Air Transport Manager, training in Belfast and Cranfield, then moving to Berkshire for a job with British Airways.

Below: The Cunninghams' prayer letter

Opposite top to bottom: The Cunningham family in the 1970s; Andrew Cunningham as a boy in Ethiopia; Andrew Cunningham (left) meets Pilot Les Brown (right)

" PRAY WITHOUT DOUBTING "
1 TIM. 2, 8

400,000 sq. miles

Population 22,500,000

RONALD, MARIA, SAMUEL and ANDREW

Postal address: P.O. BATIE, WOLLO PROVINCE, ETHIOPIA

Attending an evening service at a local church one Sunday in 2003, Andrew felt God preparing him for a new season of mission service. Driving to work the next morning, he prayed.

'I felt blown away,' he remembers. 'Sensing that only God could open a door for me to serve in mission, I asked Him to move in a way that was evident and amazing. Then, as soon as I opened my emails, there was one from our Christian Fellowship at British Airways. MAF was looking for Trustees.'

Andrew served on MAF UK's board for ten years. 'It was an absolute privilege,' he says. 'It had a real sense of being God's providential work because this was the organisation that saved my life.'

As a Trustee, Andrew was asked to speak at an event in Scotland. 'I remember sitting near an older gentleman,' says Andrew. 'We didn't chat, but after I shared my story and returned to my seat, he leaned over. "I was the pilot," he said.'

Meeting Les Brown – who flew with MAF for eleven years in Ethiopia and Kenya – spoke volumes to Andrew.

'The fact that God led us to meet was truly amazing,' he smiles. 'I was tingling all over. It touched me that he would remember that flight more than 30 years later. It shows how wonderful MAF pilots are. It was such a beautiful moment. MAF truly is an amazing, holistic, Godly mission.' ✝

COUNTRY PROFILE:
TANZANIA

The United Republic of Tanzania is a land of great diversity and beauty. Comprising the mainland of Tanganyika and the island of Zanzibar, Tanzania boasts a variety of bountiful lakes, dense forests and scenic coastlines. Home to Africa's tallest and most famous mountain peak, thousands of tourists are attracted to climb Kilimanjaro and stay in its magnificent foothills every year.

Gaining independence from Britain in 1961, Tanzania has made notable progress towards development and democracy, with economic growth fuelled by vast natural resources and a growing tourism industry. However, poverty is still widespread and almost 90% of Tanzanian children are still deprived of adequate housing and sanitation.

Across Tanzania's vast and varied landscape, many rural communities are isolated due to a limited road transport system. During wet seasons, some villages can be cut off for months at a time. With almost 80% of the workforce reliant on the agricultural sector, many families are vulnerable to the impacts of climate change, with drought and flooding frequently ruining crops and causing starvation for millions of people.

Having flown intermittently into Tanzania from Nairobi, Kenya during the 1960s, MAF considered a more regular service in Dodoma in Tanzania, as demand for flights in Kenya slowed down.

At the invitation of Bishop Yohana Madinda, Stuart King and Bob Gordon conducted an official survey of Tanzania in 1975, finding that the Church had grown significantly and had the potential to expand even further through President Julius Nyerere's African socialist model.

Seizing the opportunity, Bishop Yohana called on MAF to help the remaining *Ujamaa* villages, not yet reached with the Gospel – his whole diocese was more than 500 miles wide, with only a handful of vehicles. The need for MAF was urgent and clear.

During the early 1980s, the Church in Tanzania grew by 50% each year as *Ujamaa* villages expanded. MAF was instrumental in supporting local evangelists and missionaries, setting up regular 'safari' flight services to transport key passengers around a network of remote villages that would take many weeks to reach by land.

Half a century after MAF began serving the people of Tanzania, a comprehensive review was launched in 2014, as road networks improved and development in some rural areas seemed sustainable. MAF decided to streamline operations, while continuing to support areas of acute vulnerability from bases in Arusha and Mbeya.

Today, MAF continues to run regular medical and evangelistic safari flights, helping mission workers, development specialists and medical staff access the hardest-to-reach places. In the last decade alone, MAF has helped construct over two-dozen remote airstrips and is recognised by district hospitals, international aid agencies and the Church as providing a vital, safe service to help those with the greatest needs. ✈

African socialism, known as *Ujamaa* meaning 'oneness and familyhood', saw millions of tribespeople relocate to pool resources and work together, sharing food, water and healthcare services. Six thousand new *Ujamaa* villages were established in the 1970s, with new mud-brick houses and corrugated iron roofs. These new dwellings were made accessible not only to the government, but also the growing Church of Tanzania.

Main: Meserani, Tanzania

Opposite page: Village buildings in Malambo

COUNTRY STATS

👤 **POPULATION**
58.5 million

☆ **CAPITAL**
Dodoma

💬 **LANGUAGES**
Swahili, English,
Arabic + more than
100 indigenous
dialects

☀ **CLIMATE**
Tropical with two
rainy seasons

🗠 **LIFE EXPECTANCY**
62 years

🚩 **ROADS**
54,420 miles,
mostly unpaved
(245,000 in the UK)

🚩 **MAF AIRSTRIPS**
36

🔗 **MAF PARTNERS**
21 organisations

✈ **FLEET**
3 x Cessna 206

TIMELINE

1959 MAF's first flight into Tanzania
from Kenya

1960 MAF flies Billy Graham to Moshi,
Tanzania – 5,000 conversions
recorded

1961 Independence from Britain

1962 MAF registered to officially operate in
Tanzania with a temporary base
at Dodoma

1963 First MAF flight to take off and land in
Tanzania

1975 Survey of Tanzania, MAF aircraft and
pilot relocated from Nairobi, Kenya
to Dodoma

1977 MAF programme officially launched
in Dodoma

1978 MAF's aircraft hangar built in
Dodoma

1985 MAF begins safari flights to reach the
northern Maasai tribes

2014 Following a thorough evaluation,
MAF's services relocate to Arusha
and Mbeya to better serve those with
the greatest needs

2017 New airstrip opened at Matongo

Tanzania

CAN YOU GIVE INJECTIONS?

'Peter, did I ever show you how to give an injection?' enquired the doctor suddenly.

MAF Pilot Peter Empson had flown Dr Sam Cannata to a clinic 10,000 feet above sea level in the Ethiopian mountains. To reach the clinic, Peter had landed on a 900-yard strip and passed on foot through the marketplace, thronged with donkeys, mules and hundreds of people buying grain, spices, yarn, clay pots and blocks of salt.

The clinic was less colourful, a small, dark room with mud walls and a corrugated roof. The usual huddle of sick people waited on one side of the room, with more beginning to flock round the door and window. Peter's job was normally to sit behind a table, count tablets and hand them to patients as directed by the Ethiopian Government Nurse. But the nurse was not present today. They were on their own.

Peter glanced at his watch and wondered how Dr Cannata would possibly manage to get through all the patients. Of course, he must do everything he could to help.

'Negative,' Peter gulped, as calmly as he could.

'Well, we'll soon put that right,' was Dr Cannata's cheerful, confident response.

Within five minutes, Peter's demonstration was over, and he found himself injecting some sterile water into a bottle of penicillin powder. 'Rather like making custard,' Peter thought to himself.

'Here is your first one, Peter. 2ccs of Bicillin,' Dr Cannata shouted through the gauze curtain as a local man pushed into the room. With a shaky smile, Peter indicated for the patient to sit on the bench, coaxing some of the 'custard' into the syringe.

Eventually the clinic was over and the men returned to the plane. Bumping over the turf and accelerating into take-off, Peter was grateful to be airborne.

As the people and huts diminished in size to that of small mushrooms clustered precariously along ridges, Peter realised he had just seen those well-enough to make the long trip to the plateau top, eight treacherous miles from another village below.

'One million people to one doctor in perhaps the most inaccessible mountain fortress anywhere,' Peter wrote later.

'It would be easy to get discouraged at the impossible task of bringing healing to all those sick and dying. Yet it is not just the aim of the doctor to bring medical help to the people. We are seeing the deeper, spiritual need of those who are totally ignorant of the new peace and well-being of soul which lasts even beyond death to eternity.' ✝

Opposite, top to bottom:
The Empson family; Dr Sam Cannata; Plane landing uphill on mountain slope airstrip

LOCATION PROFILE:
ARNHEM LAND

Located in the northeast corner of Australia's Northern Territory, the region of Arnhem Land is a legally-recognised reserve for the Yolŋu people people. On a map of Australia, the area appears relatively small, but in fact measures 37,000 square miles – the size of Scotland and Wales combined.

Before the arrival of Europeans in the early 1800s, the Aborigines of northern Australia had been self-sufficient, trading sea cucumbers, pearls and turtle shells with cloth, knives and rice from Makassan traders in Indonesia.

When British colonial authorities declared all of Australia *terra nullius*, belonging to no one, massive social and economic upheaval caused clashes among the Yolŋu and other indigenous groups. The effects of this disruption are still widely felt today, and Arnhem Land exhibits many characteristics of an impoverished region, within the borders of a developed country.

Arnhem Land's vast geography and prolonged wet season hamper development efforts – the volume of rainfall across the region can be triple the amount London experiences in a year. The differences between the health of Australia's indigenous and non-indigenous groups are alarming. With the life-expectancy of Aborigines over a decade lower than that of other Australians. Having lost much of their identity, purpose and hope, in recent decades indigenous groups such as the Yolŋu have developed a range of social problems such as alcohol abuse, crime, depression and suicide.

Christian aviation in Arnhem Land dates to the 1930s, when Reverend Harold Shepherdson built a single-seater 'Health Parasol' aircraft, using a kit of parts imported from the USA. Many years later, two MAF pilots flew to Elcho Island, and met Mr Shepherdson to discuss taking his aviation mission forward.

MAF assumed responsibility of the operation at Elcho Island in 1973, and a sub-base began at Gove Airport to serve Yolŋu communities to the east. During the subsequent 20 years, MAF's work and influence has expanded considerably, with new routes connecting isolated communities to vital resources such as food, education and healthcare.

During 2010, a spirit of revival swept over Arnhem Land and MAF enabled evangelists to reach remote areas. In over 60 days of Christian outreach, preachers, musicians and ministers ran evangelistic meetings and many Yolŋu came to Christ.

Today, MAF is the only air service with permanent access to the region, which is strictly controlled to protect the traditional indigenous communities. Access to basic healthcare, fresh produce and economic opportunities is restricted for many Yolŋu homelands and MAF is working to bring about development, education and hope.

Enhancing the ability of the scattered homelands to support themselves is vital to the Yolŋu's physical and spiritual wellbeing. MAF maintains a busy programme with direct involvement from indigenous people, with half of the aircraft being owned by the Yolŋu themselves. Responding to direct requests from homeland communities, MAF staff in Arnhem Land regularly lead evangelistic outreach, support Bible translation work and have become adopted into the traditional kinship system.

Regular MAF flights support initiatives to produce locally-grown food, presenting a healthy alternative to the longer-lasting, processed products which many Yolŋu depend on, owing to limited access to fresh produce. The epidemic in type-2 diabetes which has claimed so many lives is being managed and communities are receiving education about basic healthcare and sustainability. ✛

Opposite:
Homeland
outreach in
Garrthalala

LOCATION STATS

👤 POPULATION
16,230

☆ SERVICE HUB
Nhulunbuy

💬 LANGUAGES
Hundreds of indigenous languages

⎓ LIFE EXPECTANCY
72 years

☀ CLIMATE
Tropical monsoon; one long rainy season

🚩 MAF AIRSTRIPS
56

🔗 MAF PARTNERS
91 organisations

✚ FLEET
1 x Cessna 208
9 x GA-8 Airvans

Nhulunbuy

ARNHEM LAND

AUSTRALIA

TIMELINE

○ **1930s** Rev Harold Shepherdson operates single mission aircraft

○ **1973** MAF programme launched on Elcho Island

○ **1975** Sub-base established at Gove Airport (now Nhulunbuy)

○ **1983** MAF granted Supplementary Airline Licence for scheduled services on a Cessna 402 aircraft

○ **1993** A Cessna 206 aircraft joins the fleet

○ **1995** Three aircraft and two properties establish Yolŋu's own airline

○ **2006** MAF hands its regular public transport Routes to Aboriginal Air Services

○ **2010** Christian revival in Arnhem Land, many come to Christ

○ **2017** MAF receives Air Operator's Certificate, enabling Yolŋu to book individual flights rather than entire charters

> " I have never been to fellowship before but tonight I was drawn here for some reason. Drugs, alcohol, break-ins; you name it, I have done it but I know it's not right. I have heard of Jesus, but tonight I must give my life to Him."

Young Aboriginal man sharing after an MAF outreach event

Arnhem Land

PRAYER ON THE CHECKLIST

Checklists are a part of every pilot's working life. Yet MAF's flight checklist is different from those of commercial airlines: item three is prayer.

Prayer has been a part of MAF's existence from the beginning. MAF archives document how the founders of MAF in the UK, the USA and Australia were all committed to prayer in seeking God's guidance every step of the way in research, decision making and planning. While God has endowed each person with gifts and skills – like flying a plane or aircraft maintenance – there are still factors beyond human control.

Christians put their trust in a God who is omnipotent and omniscient; whose love is immeasurable and whose mission is for His love to be taken to the ends of the earth. MAF's purpose is to share God's love through aviation and technology in the name of Jesus. Success is only possible through staying in close relationship with God. Through prayer God reveals his plans and purposes. To neglect prayer would lead to failure.

MAF and its affiliates have occasionally flown celebrities – Bob Geldof, following up the Ethiopian famine 10 years after Live Aid and Stephen Fry, when he broke his arm while filming in the Amazon. Both found it disconcerting when their pilots prayed ahead of the flight.

Handling cultural differences is a daily occurrence for MAF staff. On the subject of prayer, there is a difference between secular and Christian thinking; in western society, where many might only pray in desperation, hearing a pilot pray before take-off could cause concern. For a Christian, the context and reason for prayer is different.

MAF pilots are highly trained and professionally qualified.

Main: PK-MAF is dedicated in Sentani, Papua, Indonesia

Below: Melvin Peters prays with his children before they fly to Nairobi

They are also Christians. So why do MAF pilots pray?

At the heart of Christianity is a proactive God who has gone to great lengths, through Jesus Christ, to express love and connect with humanity. A Christian lives in relationship with God, prayer being both a response to God and also the two-way communication required for any healthy relationship. Christians seek to invest their time and effort in God's purposes rather than pursuing a life of independence. Praying before each flight is an expression of this.

MAF leadership still earnestly seek God in prayer. MAF teams across the world meet daily to pray and commit the work to the Lord. Prayer continues to be a key part of MAF's ministry. ✤

Proverbs 16:3

'Commit your work to the LORD, and your plans will be established.'

CHAD TILLEY

'I pray before every single flight. When I pray, I thank the Lord for His provision of the amphibious plane and the opportunity to serve the people of Bangladesh with such an awesome tool. In a country where the weather is frequently overcast and wet, I also pray for wisdom while flying.'

MAX GOVE

'I prayed for safety – as I do in other scenarios, such as travelling on the roads. I did my bit professionally in the plane, but I still wanted protection from other factors such as birds, air traffic mistakes, or animals running out on the airstrip.'

EMIL KUNDIG

'This item on the checklist reminds me of the opportunity to pray for the country, the work of MAF, and the work of the people we fly. For me, it has always been a privilege, during my time in Madagascar for example, to pray for the country when it was in turmoil.'

COUNTRY PROFILE:
LESOTHO

The Kingdom of Lesotho is one of only three independent states completely surrounded by the territory of another country: in this case, South Africa. Previously named *Basutoland* as part of the British empire, Lesotho was renamed when it gained independence in 1966.

Sometimes called 'the Kingdom in the Sky', the nation is covered in rocky mountains with the lowest point still rising 4,583 feet above sea level. The rugged landscape is made up of tiny, often inaccessible, villages.

The few available roads are in poor condition and make overland travel unsafe and tedious. Nearly half of all the native Basotho people are unemployed, and more than a third of men have left the country seeking employment in mining or agricultural sectors in South Africa.

This small African nation has been plagued by years of poverty and famine and has some of the highest cases of HIV/AIDS anywhere in the world. Due to persistent drought resulting in widespread famine, the people of Lesotho depend on assistance from the international community in the form of food aid. According to UNICEF, more than 1 in 3 children are orphans and 57% of people live below the poverty line.

> ## "
> **MAF continues to provide a regular, dependable service to some of the most isolated parts of the country.**

MAF's first response to Lesotho's acute needs was in 1978, when a team conducted emergency food relief flights in the highlands, leading to a long-term partnership with the Lesotho Flying Doctor Programme.

Today, MAF continues to provide a regular, dependable service to some of the most isolated parts of the country.

Alongside a more recent initiative to fly local pastors to plant and nurture rural churches, MAF's predominant work is enabling medical assistance across the rugged landscape; flying doctors to mountain clinics, transporting emergency medical cases and enabling medical staff to arrive quickly and safely where there would otherwise be no access to healthcare. ✠

Main: Aerial scenery of Lesotho, winter

Right: Isolated village

Opposite, top to bottom: Children painting; Cessna 206 on airstrip

COUNTRY STATS

👤 **POPULATION**
1.96 million

☆ **CAPITAL**
Maseru

💬 **LANGUAGES**
Sesotho, English,
Zulu, Xhosa

☀ **CLIMATE**
Temperate; cool,
dry winters and hot,
wet summers

〰 **LIFE EXPECTANCY**
53 years

🚩 **ROADS**
5,940 – mostly
unpaved (245,000
in the UK)

🚩 **MAF AIRSTRIPS**
22

🔗 **MAF PARTNERS**
14 organisations

✈ **FLEET**
4 x Cessnsa 206

SOUTH
AFRICA

☆ Maseru
LESOTHO

COUNTRY TIMELINE

- **1978** MAF's first flights offering food aid
- **1979** Partnership formed with Flying Doctor Programme
- **1980** MAF Programme launched
- **2003** MAF begins a 3-year project to combat AIDS and support local farming
- **2010** MAF employs a local chaplain to pray and minister to patients passing through the hangar
- **2015** MAF launches a Flying Pastors Programme to foster rural evangelism
- **2019** A patient guest house opens to provide a place for the sick and injured to stay

❝ Because of MAF, we get here and we're not tired. The same day we start going from village to village, so it's a really great help."

Makopi Shoaepane
Local evangelist

New Cessna 210 added to
the fleet in **Tanzania**

Chad programme reopens

New MAF hangar opened in
Dodoma, **Tanzania**

MAF begins famine relief efforts in **Ethiopia**

First **European** MAF conference

MAF **Sudan** forced to close due
to government restrictions

MAF opens a base in **Mali** in
response to African famine

MAF survey in **Mozambique**

MAF responds to **Chad** famine

1980   1981   1982   1983   1984   1985

5

THE 1980s

In the 1980s MAF responds to opportunities and challenges.

As word spread about MAF's lifesaving work, Stuart King and other MAF representatives began visiting different countries across Europe to kick-start new groups. By 1982, MAF's first European conference was launched, bringing together newly-recruited representatives from Finland, The Netherlands, Germany, Norway, Sweden, Switzerland and the UK.

Crippling famine swept across Africa, triggering a widespread disaster response effort. MAF aircraft and pilots worked around the clock to bring help to those in greatest need, using additional funds which flooded in following first-time footage captured by the BBC. Challenges continued in Sudan, with the eventual need for MAF to close the programme due to political instability. With two new programmes in Africa, MAF continued to expand its reach, reputation and lifesaving credentials.

MAF **Kenya** establishes sub-base in Kampala with a Cessna 210

MAF **Norway** formed

MAF **Haiti** programme launched

MAF **Uganda** programme launched

MAF **Madagascar** programme launched

MAF **Denmark** formed

MAF **Canada** launches a programme in **Angola**

1986   **1987** **1988** **1989**

AIRSTRIP OPENING:
A WORLD LONG PRAYED-FOR

A first-hand account from MAF Pilot Max Chapman, Papua New Guinea, 1981.

Checks completed and lined up – full throttle – watch the fuel flow, bring it back an inch.

I ease back on the control column and there's the new sensation that overtakes me – flight. Looking back, the huge white runway markings are left behind as is the rest of the sophistication of our scientific age. Just 50 minutes later we are in the world of yesteryear, the far outpost at April River, PNG.

For the last two years I have flown over this area of winding rivers and endless jungle. Often driven by an urge within me to be part of that scene too, to encourage those labouring in excessive heat with their joys and disappointments, I'd throttle back to dip a wing, then a prayer of praise before heading on to my destination somewhere in the Highlands.

But now it's grand opening day for this remote village.

Circling around the landing area, we search for obstacles; pigs, dogs or even people themselves. Banking now, on to final approach.

Strip still clear ahead, throttling back, we glide into short final, sparing a glance at the forest's giants on either side with their outstretched limbs. We must concentrate on keeping right down the centre of the approach path if we are to make it to the threshold. The chattering

Bottom:
P2-MFF, a
Cessna 185, at
April River

Opposite: A
community
served by the
airstrip

of the undercarriage as we touch on the grassy sod alerts us to the reality of our arrival.

Immediately surrounded by 150 whooping, over-excited warriors, wives and children, all in full paint and head-dress, could make one just a little nervous. The brilliant crown of bird-of-paradise plumes and the painted bodies with weapons in hand, welcomes a world long prayed-for, but just opening to the glorious light of the Gospel. ✈

CHAD FAMINE

When MAF returned to Chad in 1981, its people were still recovering from the effects of war, leaving them weak and impoverished.

Below and opposite, top: MAF provide food and healing in response to famine in Chad

Opposite, bottom: Locust and grasshopper plague; Crop-spraying by to save a harvest

Poor rainfall in the early 1980s made survival even harder as crops began to fail. In 1985, thousands of Chadians left their homes in search of food, making a perilous 1,000-mile journey to cross the border into Darfur, Sudan. In spite of this, hundreds of children were dying each day.

In the south of Chad, MAF was flying regularly to 32 dispensaries in the Bébalém district and was discovering first-hand the devastating consequence of the lack of rain, which had caused the rice crop to fail. Unless urgent action was taken, 30,000 people in the villages that MAF served would

die of starvation.

MAF supporters generously responded to an appeal for funds and a relief operation was set up involving MAF, local Chadians, churches and mission workers, including the hospital at Bébalém.

Thankfully, late rains saved some crops further in the south and there was grain to spare, which the MAF team bought and stored at Andoum. Meanwhile, one of the mission houses at Bébalém was converted into a grain store to receive the tonnes of millet, rice, beans and wheat that were ferried there by MAF planes.

Local Chadians worked

tirelessly to fill sacks with these supplies, which MAF then distributed to villages, avoiding bandits that still roamed the area.

Running alongside the food distribution was a vaccination and health education programme, designed to provide additional help to those already badly malnourished.

As the number of villages needing help increased, MAF gathered an emergency task force of additional staff and extra aircraft were loaned from other MAF programmes to help meet the demand for flights.

By the end of the operation 2,460 tonmes of grain had been distributed, helping to save

the lives of 55,000 people and 1,600 children were vaccinated, averting a measles epidemic.

A further benefit to MAF's disaster response programme in Chad was that people were able to stay in their homes, avoiding refugee camps and subsequent resettlement, so villagers were in the right place to plant their crops the following year.

Two years later, in 1987, MAF helped avert another famine in Chad when a massive locust and grasshopper plague threatened to ruin an entire harvest. MAF adapted one of its aircraft for crop-spraying and acquired two other specialist planes, enabling it to treat 320,000 acres of land in less than 2 months. ✈

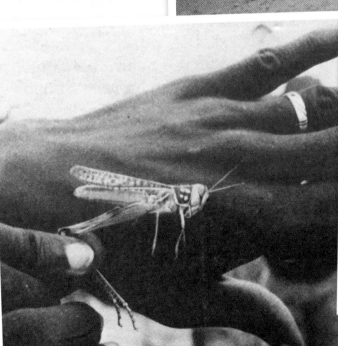

KNOWING GOD'S GUIDANCE

Case Study: Max Gove

From the very first flight, MAF pilots have sought to use the best navigational tools available.

For Stuart King and Jack Hemmings these were a map and compass which worked wonders in their skilled hands!

Over the years, navigational tools have evolved, increasingly becoming electronic and now MAF uses GPS satellite technology to pin point locations enabling MAF aircraft, pilots and passengers to steer accurately to their destinations. However, these are not all MAF pilots use to determine direction.

God's Navigational Tools

For MAF and the people who have dedicated their lives to service in His name, God's guidance is equally, if not more, important; especially when it comes to new initiatives.

But what are the navigational tools that the

Proverbs 3:5-6

Trust in the LORD with all your heart; and lean not on your own understanding;

In all your ways submit to him and he will make your paths straight.

Right: Max Gove in Ethiopia in the mid 1970s

Opposite, top to bottom: Max and Sue Gove with two of their daughters; MAF Pilot Max Gove

Lord has used to guide MAF over the years?

The experience of Max Gove, currently an MAF UK Trustee, illustrates the different ways God has guided MAF over the years.

Prior to his retirement, Max and his wife Sue served for 43 years with MAF after Max first heard a call to overseas mission at the tender age of 7.

The advice of his father, a pastor, was to receive clear guidance from God for any situation and, having received guidance, never revisit it. Max has wisely and faithfully followed this advice during his time with MAF.

Max affirms that prayer, circumstances, meticulous research, previous experience and an overwhelming sense of God's peace all play a vital part and have been blended together in the wisdom of God to lead and guide MAF into new ventures as well as closing some doors.

At only 14 years of age, Max had his first interview with Steve Stevens in MAF UK's office and met Stuart King, who, impressed with this passion for mission, advised him on what subjects to study to become an MAF Pilot.

While still only 18, a financial loan became available for flight training and so Max enrolled at the Bedfordshire School of Flying at Cranfield, Bedford.

Max's first assignment with MAF was in Ethiopia, arriving there in March 1972 with his wife Sue. Max was immediately responsible for the operation of one aircraft which carried supplies and people to more than 80 airstrips.

Six months later Max and Sue relocated to Jimma, Ethiopia where Max became responsible for the upkeep of airstrip records for the whole country. This included trekking into new airstrips to inspect them and ensure they were safe before the first landing of an MAF plane.

In 1974 there was a military coup in

Ethiopia and, while initially mission work and MAF's support of these services was able to continue, by 1976, life in Ethiopia was very unsettled. Many missions had been forced to leave rural areas and the number of MAF flights declined significantly, so in 1977, MAF took the difficult decision to leave Ethiopia and Max and his family returned to the UK.

Max and Sue continued to seek God's guidance in this sad and confusing time and were clearly led to return to Africa, this time to Kenya. Max first served there as a pilot, later becoming the Kenyan MAF Programme Manager, based in Nairobi.

This was a time of significant change for MAF operations in Africa and Max not only oversaw the opening of three new sub-bases in Tanzania, he also worked in co-operation with MAF-USA on a joint venture which opened up new routes into Zaire, Central African Republic, Sudan, Somalia, Tanzania, Uganda and The Union of the Comoros.

In 1984, Max and his family returned to the UK where he took up the role of Director of Overseas Operations with MAF UK. In 1991, Max was appointed Chief Executive Officer (CEO) of MAF UK and in 1994, he was appointed as CEO of MAF Europe.

Following a 12-month study sabbatical, Max's role changed again in 1996, when he became Special Projects Manager, using his extensive skills and experience of overseas

mission to 'spy out the land' for new MAF programmes, opening new ventures and developing existing programmes. This included initiatives in Chad, Madagascar, Mongolia, Bangladesh, Namibia, Nepal, Cambodia, Timor-Leste, South Sudan, South Africa, Ethiopia and Liberia.

Max recalls how a sense of God's peace was crucial in determining the right course of action when MAF was looking to begin work in Mongolia.

'I was in my hotel room in Mongolia, trying to work out how MAF should be established there. I knew it wasn't my decision, but God's. I called out, 'God, YOU have to show me what to do'. By nightfall, I experienced an incredible peace as God had given me the answer, which was a joint venture with Mongolian Christian Businessmen which would last for the next 20 years until the programme closed in 2020'.

From the early days of identifying and securing safe airstrips in Ethiopia, to overseeing joint ventures in Nairobi, finally researching opportunities for new ventures and negotiating terms for brand new programmes, Max has sought to know the mind of God.

In doing so, the Kingdom of God has made significant advance. ✠

PRAYER, PEOPLE AND PROVISION

Stuart King would often comment on the simultaneous beginnings of MAF around the world as clearly being led by God: 'as we didn't have email in those days!'

Clockwise from top right:

Current MAF logo used globally

MAF Worldwide map, from MAF News, Jan 1982

MAF Europe logo

An early MAF logo

Stuart King and Betty Greene in Sudan, early 1950s

Bringing people together with a common purpose and vision has seen different stages of development over the years. The birth of the vision led to US based, British based and Australian MAF Groups being established in the 1940's and, as early as 1948, a merger was considered.

International collaboration has always been important, using informal networking and international conferences to develop protocols and seek the Lord together.

MAF Groups then began opening up in other European countries in the 1970s. In 1976, Christians in Finland began to recruit staff to second to MAF programmes. In 1978, MAF Netherlands was formed with a similar remit. Christians and missions in Sweden, Germany, Switzerland, Denmark and Norway began to follow suit, with some raising funds for new aircraft.

These new MAF Groups all had a common goal. The ethos of 'separate but seen as one' was a guiding principle for collaboration and a shared partnership in the Gospel underwrote informal relationships.

In the 1980s, long term strategic planning recognised the need to develop and strengthen links between all the MAF organisations.

In 1982 MAF held its first annual European MAF conference with representatives from each of the European MAF Groups and the following year established a European Co-ordinating Committee to explore how the different entities could best work together and how their different perspectives and experiences could be combined.

Meanwhile, MAF Canada had been formed in 1973 with close connections to MAF USA, but there was increasing contact with MAF in the UK. They had provided finance for a hangar in Sudan and links strengthened as staff were seconded to many overseas programmes.

While the MAF US, MAF Canada and MAF UK Groups

Above and Beyond

independently managed the different MAF Country programmes, the MAF teams in Africa and Asia Pacific worked closely together.

The work of the European Co-ordinating Committee continued apace, considering various ways the different entities could most effectively work together and share resources.

In June 1986, representatives from Canada, Finland, The Netherlands and Sweden joined discussions about working more closely together.

A new MAF Europe board was officially constituted in 1989 and, five years later, MAF Europe was re-constituted to focus on overseas operations and operational assets, including 30 aircraft, were transferred to MAF Europe. The European Groups, including MAF UK, became Resourcing Groups, focusing on mobilising and gathering the necessary resources of people, prayer and pounds for MAF operations.

During this time, MAF South Africa, MAF New Zealand, MAF Australia, MAF USA and MAF Canada continued as autonomous national organisations but worked in co-operation with each other and MAF Europe, especially regarding the secondment of staff and in disaster response, the loan of aircraft and technical support.

Nevertheless, closer co-operation continued to be explored and in 2006, MAF Europe was reconstituted as MAF International, in order to incorporate MAF's operations in Africa and Asia Pacific. At this point, MAF Australia, MAF New Zealand, MAF Canada and MAF South Africa joined MAF International as members. MAF USA and MAF International continue to work closely and strategically to maximise their impact for global mission.

For 75 years, the 'family' of MAF has expanded and continues to expand with new Resourcing Groups in Asia now also generating the three 'P's of prayer, people and provision.

Today, global co-operation continues at operational and strategic level. MAF members see themselves as inter-dependent groups working together with a common vision, purpose and calling. ✈

In 2012, an MAF global task force explored the desire for a common global logo and developed a brand to represent the unity of the mission of MAF to all who support and are served by MAF worldwide.

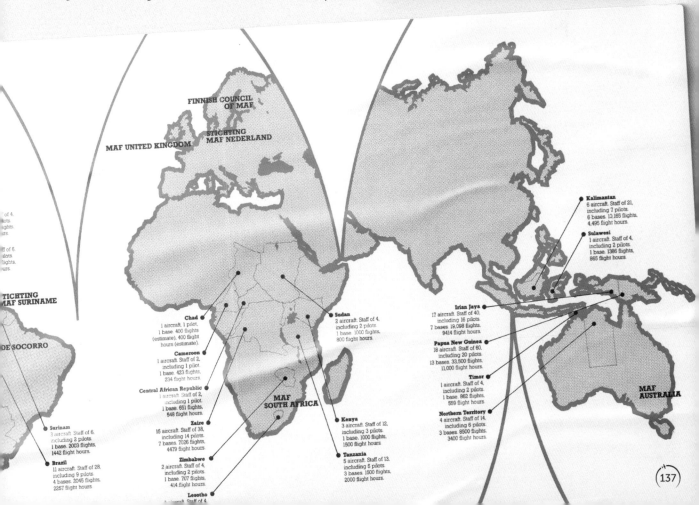

DISASTER RESPONSE
INDONESIAN EARTHQUAKE

When MAF Pilot David Marfleet arrived in Papua, Indonesia in 1982, he experienced first-hand the difficulty of reaching isolated tribes in a country dominated by mountains and jungles.

Below: Earthquake casualty

Opposite top: Only a helicopter could land on the damaged strip

Opposite right: David Marfleet returns to Papua in December 2014 and meets Diana

Opposite right: Diana's village at Sebu Ridge, Soba 2014

As Indonesia lies within the Pacific Ring of Fire, where several tectonic plates intersect, there are frequently additional problems caused by earthquakes, which reinforce the country's reputation as having some of the toughest flying in the world.

On 1 August 1989, David was already airborne in a Cessna 185 aircraft when he received a call from missionary nurse, Sue Trenier, near an airstrip at Soba, Papua. Her house was being shaken off its foundations by an earthquake and mud was pouring down the valley. As the airstrip had developed three large cracks, it wasn't possible for David to land, so he diverted to Wamena to pick up one of MAF's helicopters which could land on the damaged strip.

When he arrived at the valley he was aghast at the destruction: There had been massive landslides and mudslides up to 200 metres high and 4 villages were almost completely destroyed. Fresh tremors and aftershocks continued to shake rocks free that rolled down the valley causing even more damage.

He was joined by MAF's other helicopter pilot, American Mike Meeuwse and they quickly agreed a plan of action, focused on rescuing the injured. They took one side of the valley each, so they could both airlift the injured to Sue at Soba for triage and first aid. The injured were then ferried them to hospital via Passema, in Sumatra, using MAF's fixed wing aircraft.

David and Mike had to duck under low cloud cover into the valley where enormous dust clouds from the earthquake seriously hampered visibility, which became worse when smoke from fires mingled with the dust.

The rescue operation was dangerous and required immense skill. On the steep mountainsides, there was nowhere flat to land: David had to put one skid on a rock and hold the helicopter steady while a rescue worker jumped out to haul people in to safety. All the while, the helicopter blades were often only 18 inches from the mountainside, and large rocks were crashing down around them.

David and Mike worked relentlessly for several days, looking for survivors and rescuing hundreds of Hupla tribespeople.

Eventually, the rescue operation gradually shifted into a series of flights bringing much needed relief.

When David left Papua a year later, MAF was still flying in tonnes of food for the survivors but some village dwellings and vegetable gardens had been restored: a wonderful sign of hope.

25 years later, Hupla village elders were planning a celebration to mark the dedication of 5,000 copies of the newly translated Bible in the Hupla language.

They remembered 'the pilot who loved us' and so invited David and his wife Mary back as honoured guests at the celebrations.

Among those David met was a lady called Diana. She exclaimed: 'I was only seven years old and had lost my parents when our hut fell down the mountain. I was alone on the mudslide, but you came and lifted me to safety!'

At the celebration, David read from the book of Ecclesiastes, Chapter 3, saying: 'the last time we were here, we had to mourn with you. But now, 25 years later, we've returned, to dance with you!' ✝

COUNTRY PROFILE:
MADAGASCAR

The Republic of Madagascar was one of the last major habitable landmasses on earth to be settled by humans. A convenient trading post for Arab and Persian merchants, the island was used as a pirate stronghold and slave-trading centre, finally conquered by the French in 1896.

Eventual independence in 1960 brought political turbulence and a struggle for democracy, with the benefits of recent economic growth barely improving living standards for most people. Despite boasting a wealth of natural resources including minerals and an incredibly diverse plant life, Madagascar is among the least-developed countries in the world.

Portrayed in Western magazines as an exotic tourist destination, behind its idyllic, white sandy beaches, close to 80% of Madagascar's population are barely surviving on less than £1.40 a day. Only 13% of households have access to electricity, and millions of the Malagasy people are affected by the severe cyclones, which wipe out crops and dwellings every single year in this island country.

Booming birth rates in recent years have led to alarming levels of deforestation because lush rainforests have been replaced by rice fields, in order that farmers can provide for their growing families. Young women are sold as wives and give birth before the age of 18, going on to have three or more children, on average.

There is almost no access to basic healthcare. Terrible roads, tremendous stretches of thick rainforests and imposing, rugged mountains stand between those of Madagascar's population who are sick and life-saving medical treatment. With almost half of Malagasy children under the age of five suffering malnutrition, there is no place more in need of an air service. Today, thousands of communities continue to rely on aid provided by NGOs, churches and mission agencies to survive and MAF's aircraft are often the only way they can be reached.

Responding to requests from missionaries in Madagascar, MAF first surveyed the island in 1975, identifying a great and immediate need for its services. However, political instability rendered MAF's applications unsuccessful and it wasn't until 1985 that a second survey was conducted at the invitation of the American Lutheran Mission, who desperately needed help to distribute their medical teams to remote communities.

Finally receiving government permission in 1988, the first MAF plane and pilot arrived in the capital Antananarivo and the passenger lists quickly expanded from Church organisations to several NGOs and humanitarian causes, who could now travel quickly and safely across the island. MAF's presence came at a critical stage in the country's development and has been relied on ever since.

Today, thousands of aid workers, long-term development specialists, government officials, mission workers and medics depend on MAF to enable them to work effectively. MAF flights support food production projects, hygiene initiatives, medical outreaches, evangelistic outreaches and education programmes to help improve life for the most vulnerable.

MAF has also made a long-term commitment to the development of the country by employing and training national staff in a variety of professional roles, including opening a dedicated maintenance workshop, which now services vehicles for many NGOs and is run by Malagasy staff. ✦

Above: Madritsara, northern Madagascar

Opposite: *Bev Erasmus of Wycliffe Bible Translators*

COUNTRY STATS

👤 **POPULATION**
25 million

⭐ **CAPITAL**
Antananarivo

☀ **CLIMATE**
Tropical coast, arid south, one cyclone season

🚩 **ROADS**
19,660 miles, mostly unpaved (245,000 in the UK)

💬 **LANGUAGES**
French, Malagasy, English

〰 **LIFE EXPECTANCY**
67.3 years

🚩 **MAF AIRSTRIPS**
55

🔗 **MAF PARTNERS**
73 organisations

✈ **FLEET**
2 x Cessna 182 SMA
1 x Cessna 208

Antananarivo

MADAGASCAR

> " MAF has been a real blessing, going out of their way many times. It's not just a little transport service, but really working hand-in-hand to find out what we need. Our teams in the east coast would need four days to travel out and that's if the roads are good. MAF has completely changed the way they work and make progress. Without MAF to fly them, I suspect a lot of them wouldn't be here."

Bev Erasmus
Wycliffe Bible Translators

TIMELINE

- **1960** Independence from France
- **1975** First survey, MAF applications unsuccessful due to political unrest
- **1985** Second survey, MAF applications received
- **1988** MAF programme launched
- **1989** Twin-engine Partenavia P68C aircraft arrives for mountain flying
- **1996** Twin-engine Partenavia Victor introduced allowing use of jet fuel
- **2003** Cessna 208 replaces the P.68C, hangar altered to accommodate it
- **2006** MAF registered as an NGO in Madagascar
- **2006** MAF invites HoverAid to partner from Antananarivo base
- **2008** Second C208 arrives
- **2011** Political unrest decreases demand, C208 redeployed to MAF in the DRC
- **2012** Cessna 182 SMA introduced due to demand for a smaller aircraft
- **2016** Second C182 SMA joins the fleet
- **2016** Madagascar Medical Safari flights reach over 8,000 remote patients

Madagascar

THE FLEET:
CESSNA 182 SMA

The basic design of the Cessna 182 SMA Skylane aircraft dates from 1956 and, like many of Cessna's aircraft models, has been progressively updated during its lifespan.

Despite the age of the C182 SMA design, MAF has only started using it in recent years; it only has four seats and a limited cargo capacity, so its bigger brother – the Cessna 206 – was always preferred.

However, the spiralling cost and reduced availability of Avgas fuel has meant that conventional piston-engined aircraft like the C206 are becoming less cost-effective. The bigger turbine-powered aircraft (like the Cessna 208 Caravan family) are suitable for large groups of passengers but can be prohibitively costly for individuals or very small groups. There is therefore still a real need for a smaller, more efficient aircraft type in some of MAF's programmes.

Main: TT-BRT in Chad

Converted to use a special diesel-type engine developed by the French company SMA, the cost-effective, Jet fuel-burning Cessna 182 SMA offers a partial solution to this problem. However, the SMA SR305-230 engine suffers from reduced power in very hot conditions, meaning that MAF's C182 SMAs in Chad and South Sudan are often limited to flying in the cooler mornings and evenings. It is also a particularly maintenance intensive powerplant, requiring overhauls at more regular intervals than conventional engines. Despite these limitations, the C182 SMA aircraft are a much-valued component of the MAF fleet, opening up flight services to a wide range of communities that might otherwise be inaccessible, or would be impossibly expensive to serve. ✈

GENERAL CHARACTERISTICS

Crew
one

Capacity
three passengers

Length
8.68m (28ft 6in)

Wingspan
10.97m (36ft)

Height
2.84m (9ft 4in)

Wing area
16.20m² (174sq. ft)

Empty weight
948kg (2,092lb)

Max. take off weight
1,633kg (3,600lb)

Powerplant
one SMA SR305-
230 diesel engine
(169kW/227hp)

Propeller
three-bladed
MT-Propeller composite
constant-speed

PERFORMANCE

Max. speed
150kn (280km/h, 170mph)

Cruise speed
145kh (269km/h, 167mph)

Stall speed
49kn (91km/h, 56mph)

Range
930nmi (1,720km, 1,070mi)

Service ceiling
18,100ft

Rate of climb
924ft/min

WHAT THE PILOT SAYS:

'The Cessna 182 SMA is a great tool, fun to fly and
economical for the passengers, allowing many
communities to be reached where it would be
financially unviable to use a larger aircraft.'

Becki Dillingham
MAF Pilot, Madagascar

AIRSTRIP OPENING:
TO THE EDGE OF THE SERENGETI

A first-hand account from MAF Pilot Peter Empson, Tanzania, 1985.

The little red and white Cessna climbed steadily, leaving the airfield at Arusha behind us. Our destination, Loliondo, was an isolated settlement in a forgotten part of Tanzania close to the border with Kenya and overlooking the Serengeti National Park.

Leaving the lush mountain slopes, the terrain changed to dry grassland. The odd herd of cattle moved slowly along well-worn tracks, kicking up great clouds of dust. But this trip was not a sight-seeing excursion. We

would be travelling by air, Land Rover and on foot to site some new airstrips in this remote Maasai region so they should hear of the love of Jesus.

As I descended, we disturbed the spectacular flamingos who clearly objected to the noise of the Cessna's engine. A four-wheel drive vehicle waited to take us ten hours (two days in the rainy season) to our overnight stop. We would be away from the aircraft for three days and, after some persuasion, a local Christian volunteered to

guard the plane from the inside – leopard and lion were in the area and no one relished the thought of being eaten during the night.

After obtaining a hunting licence, we set off south to Arash, a tiny Maasai village where there was a school and dispensary. On arrival, the teacher told us he had only a handful of children because they had left to take cattle to find grass. The failure of the rains was a big problem here.

Having carefully marked the first airstrip, we set off for

Bottom:
Pastor Lemashon, flown by MAF, speaking with Maasai

Opposite, l-r: The challenging terrain of north Tanzania;

Pastor Lemashon with Elisha Moita, 2019

our next destination, Sonjo. Stopping twice, we tried to shoot our supper but failed. On reflection it may have been that I was following too closely behind the hunter with a camera!

Light had almost gone when we caught sight of our supper – an impala. 90 minutes later we came to a little cluster of huts. Pastor Lemashon explained that the Sonjo tribe are few in number and surrounded by Maasai, who raided the village and burnt many of the homes to steal cattle some years ago. The Maasai regard all cows to be their rightful property, given by their gods.

Presenting the impala for supper, we were warmly welcomed and the women lost no time in cleaning it and preparing a fire. I held the torch.

The last day of our survey started with breakfasting on our last loaf of bread, sweet tea and leftover meat. We quickly set about siting the final airstrip, the village chairman arriving to offer his full support. He took great trouble to see exactly where the boundaries would be located.

Our work complete, we set off in the Land Rover on the long journey back to our Cessna. Finally in the air, we did a low pass over the recently sited Sonjo airstrip. This was a tremendous breakthrough in reaching the Maasai people with the Gospel. The local Church would use our aircraft each month for up to four days at a time. Pastor Lemashon could now preach Christ to his own people, just as God had called him to do. We had turned his dream into a reality. ✈

MOZAMBIQUE IS CALLING

In June 1985, pilots Tom de Waal, Art Mitchell and John Clifford from MAF Tanzania spent time in Nampula, in the far north of Mozambique to survey the needs of churches and missions there. They reported a desperate situation:

A small group of villagers huddled round the base of a mango tree. It was baking hot. In their nakedness, covered only by strips of torn sacking and caked with dried mud, it was hard to tell men from women.

These people had nothing. They had lost their homes, their livelihoods, their families.

These were the victims of an underground army called the Mozambique National Resistance or *Renamo*; labelled as a liberation movement but operating against both the military and the unarmed civilian population with massacre, robbery and brutal mutilation.

It is hard to find a Mozambiquan who has not had a relative killed or injured. It's estimated that 500,000 people have died and some five million are displaced – most don't understand the struggle and see no end to it.

Renamo rebels have maimed and mutilated hundreds of children, training them to participate in the fighting by force. Boys of 10 or 12 are given 3 weeks' military training, then made to kill a relative or neighbour. Traumatised, the children surrender to become child soldiers.

MAF considered how to respond, initially using Tanzanian-based aircraft to transport supplies and pastors to areas which are largely inaccessible.

Above: Locals cross a bridge in Mozambique

Right: Mozambique soldiers in front of an MAF C206, during military operations in Tete province

Opposite, top: Children play in front of NS494X

Opposite, bottom: Pilot Dave LePoidevin loading cargo

In the survey report, John Clifford writes: 'The Union Baptist Church has six pastors in Nampula Province – one has been kidnapped by bandits. There are about 20,000 Christians across 158 churches.

One reason for rapid growth is that the government prohibits gatherings of more than 20 people. Thus, as a congregation grows, it must split to form new ones. The pastors see their main aim as nurturing and planting these tiny fellowships. After years of being told there is no God, people are now receptive to the Gospel.

Because of the war, large areas of the province are cut off. Surface transport is impossible, but planes can fly in and out. In Nampula, 80,000 people have lost their homes and crops. 180,000 have been displaced. We visited various centres for displaced people, each had between 800 and 1,800 people building temporary dwellings out of mud. These people have lost everything.

One woman told me, "We put our babies in sacks to sleep, just like dried cassava plants." Some don't even have sacks. Food is extremely scarce and many are surviving on just leaves. Some villagers described the attacks on their homes; "We woke to gunshots and ran into the bush to escape, losing our children in the dark and confusion. We

hid for three days until the bandits had gone, only to return and find everything burnt down. We started walking to a secure town, not knowing if our children are alive or dead."

Despite the immense suffering, God is blessing His Church in Mozambique. The pastors have a real heart to share Jesus, often risking their lives on dangerous journeys by car, bicycle or foot. But they desperately need MAF's help and support.' ✠

COUNTRY PROFILE:
UGANDA

The colonial boundaries created by Britain to landlock Uganda forced a wide range of ethnic groups to muddle in together. After the country's independence in 1962, widespread cultural tensions made forming a political community extremely challenging and the rule of Idi Amin in the 1970s increased these tensions. Acute poverty and uncertainty still grips many of Uganda's rural areas.

With few good roads reaching these remote communities, many people are still cut-off from the resources they need to support themselves. According to the World Bank, for every three Ugandans who escape poverty, two fall back into it.

The 1990s saw Uganda hit news headlines again as a local militia, the Lord's Resistance Army, waged a brutal campaign of violence and terror across the region, displacing 1.8 million people. The group's leader, Joseph Kony, is still at large and the scars of his brutality remain.

Despite this civil trauma, Uganda has offered one of the most remarkable displays of hospitality in recent times – welcoming over one million refugees from South Sudan since the outbreak of violence in 2013. Vast humanitarian settlements along Uganda's northern border offer South Sudanese families a chance to rebuild their lives, yet these areas are still extremely remote and are becoming more and more entrenched in poverty.

Uganda's fertile, tropical climate give the agricultural sector huge potential and natural resources include gold, oil and copper. Farming is one of the most important sectors of the economy, employing 72% of the work force – yet lengthy journeys along dirt tracks in equatorial heat mean many farmers cannot offer their produce to larger markets before it spoils. This means that only 4% of Ugandan households have secure access to food.

MAF began flying into Uganda from neighbouring bases in the 1950s, but with fairly good infrastructure, there was little need for a permanent base there. This all changed as the country surged through a messy independence.

Setting up a sub-base in Kampala to respond to the needs of agencies working in Uganda, MAF quickly realised that an independent base was needed within the country to cater for the growing needs. Since then, the programme has continued to expand beyond expectation and has now become one of MAF's busiest African programmes.

Setting up a maintenance base at Kajjansi, the facility grew to become an entire MAF-owned airfield, attracting new tenants which now include Kampala Executive Aviation and the Police Air Wing. MAF aircraft maintenance engineers at Kajjansi service aircraft from MAF programmes in the DRC, Liberia and South Sudan and the instalment of purpose-built offices brought all the operations, finance and maintenance teams on to one, smoothly run site.

Today, MAF is recognised by the government, international aid agencies, national organisations and Churches as providing a vital, safe service for their staff and cargo. Thousands of aid workers, long-term development specialists, mission workers and medical experts have been able to provide practical help and spiritual healing to the country's most isolated communities. Weekly shuttle flights around Uganda make it economical for missions to support their work in remote, insecure areas – often places only reached by MAF's little planes. MAF's partners in Uganda describe its air service as a lifeline, not a luxury. ✈

Main: MAF Uganda's northern shuttle, Kalongo

Above: 5X-LDR in Moyo, Northern Uganda

Opposite: Baroness Cox (r)

COUNTRY STATS

👤 **POPULATION**
43.25 million

☆ **CAPITAL**
Kampala

💬 **LANGUAGES**
English, Swahili, Arabic

🚩 **ROADS**
12,765 miles, mostly unpaved (245,000 in the UK)

〰 **LIFE EXPECTANCY**
68.2 years

☀ **CLIMATE**
Tropical and rainy, with two dry seasons

🚩 **MAF AIRSTRIPS**
50

🔗 **MAF PARTNERS**
471 organisations

✛ **FLEET**
1 x Cessna 206
4 x Cessna 208

> **"** MAF's ministry makes our work in HART possible, reaching people in locations we could not visit without their superb ministry and professionalism."
>
> **Baroness Cox**
> Humanitarian Aid Relief Trust (HART)

TIMELINE

1950s MAF begins flying into Uganda from Kenya and Sudan

1962 Independence from Britain

1987 MAF Uganda programme launched

1991 Two Cessna 210 aircraft join the fleet

1994 MAF hangar built at Kajjansi for aircraft maintenance

1994 Amphibious Cessna 185 aircraft joins the fleet for use on Lake Victoria, east Africa

1995 MAF buys entire Kajjansi airfield and runway is extended

1997 A Cessna Caravan joins the fleet

2004 Amphibious aircraft discontinued due to insufficient use

2006 Second Cessna Caravan joins fleet

2009 Third Cessna Caravan joins fleet

2013 Uganda becomes a training base, a fourth Cessna Caravan aircraft arrives

2014 Cessna 182 SMA joins fleet

2015 New purpose-built offices built at Kajjansi airfield

Uganda

THE FLEET:
CESSNA 208 CARAVAN

First flown in 1982, the turbine-powered Cessna 208 Caravan family of utility aircraft is widely recognised as one of the most versatile and adaptable ever produced.

Below: Ian Purdey unloading RPT cargo at Milingimbi, off the coast of Arnhem Land

More than 2,600 Caravans have been built, and the aircraft is still being produced in an updated form today.

Cessna Caravans are a very important part of MAF's fleet, with more than 30 currently in service around the world.

MAF Caravans are modified to make them more suitable for continual use on unprepared airstrips: strengthened axles, with larger wheels and tyres are fitted; mud-guards and tyre-scrapers are added; the nose-wheel leg is replaced with a longer item, to improve propeller clearance on uneven ground; and the cargo door frame is reinforced with stainless steel strips, reducing the chance of accidental damage during loading and unloading of the aircraft.

The Caravan's cabin can be easily and quickly converted to accommodate passengers, freight, or a mixture of the two. Large loading doors at the rear of the cabin allow bulky items, such as building materials or small vehicles, to be loaded.

The majority of MAF's C208s are the 'stretched' Grand Caravan variant, which can carry a maximum of 13 passengers, or up to 1,587kg of cargo. In most regards, the Grand Caravan is the same as the original Caravan design; the key difference is that the fuselage has been extended in length by 1.21m, allowing extra carrying capacity – particularly for bulky items. The longer fuselage also allows a bigger cargo pod to be fitted, further increasing the aircraft's load capacity.

MAF also operates the 'Amphibian' Caravan model, designed to be operated from both land and water. Based upon the standard short Caravan, the main physical difference is the addition of Wipaire-manufactured floats, which feature retractable wheels and water-rudders. The aircraft's tail unit is features secondary vertical stabilisers, to improve directional stability when fitted with floats. While the amphibious version of the Caravan can still carry nine passengers, the extra drag created by the amphibious conversion has a detrimental impact on the aircraft's range and speed. However, in water-logged countries like Bangladesh, the ability to land almost anywhere on the river network hugely outweighs any minor penalty in performance. ✛

FACTFILE

GENERAL CHARACTERISTICS

Crew
one

Capacity
nine passengers

Length
11.46m (37ft 7in)

Wingspan
15.87m (52ft 1in)

Height
4.53m (14ft 11in)

Wing area
25.96m² (279sq. ft)

Empty weight
2,145kg (4,730lb)

Gross weight
3,629kg (8,000lb)

Powerplant
one Pratt & Whitney
Canada PT6A-114A
turboprop
(503kW/675shp)

Propeller
three-bladed McCauley
constant-speed, full
feathering, reversible
pitch

PERFORMANCE

Cruise speed
186kn (344km/h, 214mph)
true air speed

Stall speed
61kn (113km/h, 70mph)
calibrated air speed

Range
1,070nmi (1,982km, 1,232mi)

Service ceiling
25,000ft

Rate of climb
1,234ft/min

WHAT THE PILOT SAYS

'The C208 is a reliable, robust aircraft that is ideal for the
airstrips we fly to. It gives us the opportunity to fly to remote
airstrips as well as across international borders to serve our
partners and bridge the gap to isolated, remote communities.
As we operate regular shuttles, the C208 is economical
and ideal for our partners to book a single seat rather than
chartering the whole plane.'

Lungpinglak Domtta
MAF Pilot, Uganda

COUNTRY PROFILE:
ANGOLA

The Republic of Angola is the seventh-largest country in Africa hosting a wide variety of ethnic groups, tribes and kingdoms. Vast mineral and petroleum reserves give its economy huge potential, yet wealth is concentrated amongst a small percentage of the population. Poverty and hunger are widespread and child malnutrition rates are among the highest in the world. Sadly, fewer than half of women deliver their babies with the assistance of trained personnel and 6% of newborns die during delivery.

Independence from Portuguese rule in 1975 sparked 27 years of tragic civil war and it is thought that 1.5 million people lost their lives. Four million fled violence that tore the country apart, with at least ten million hidden landmines, wreaking havoc in rural communities. These remnants of war continue to put Angolans at risk every day.

Kalukembe Hospital, through the national church organisation Igreja Evangélica Sinodal de Angola (IESA), appealed to MAF in 1987 and, in co-operation with the Angolan government, an in-depth survey was launched to assess the feasibility and safety of flight operations. MAF Canada began the programme in Lubango, registering as an NGO in Angola. A Cessna 208 was imported and began operations in 1989.

By February 1992, increased demand for MAF flights saw a second, twin-engined King Air aircraft join the fleet, which enabled high-altitude flying at faster speeds to reduce the threat of anti-aircraft missiles and ground fire. A second base was established in the capital Luanda and, by 1996, MAF celebrated 10,000 hours of flying in Angola, with many relief flights serving the UN and the United Nations World Food Programme (WFP).

At the turn of the century, security concerns due to the ongoing civil unrest required MAF to consolidate operations to the Lubango base. The number of NGOs operating in Angola steadily declined until the eventual end of civil war in 2002. In 2012, MAF sought a smaller, cheaper aircraft to make flying more cost-effective for the national Churches and NGO partners who remained in the country, and imported two Cessna 182 SMA aircraft. These aircraft, along with the C208, still provide essential flights including a flying doctor service to remote and vulnerable areas.

Today, over four million Angolans are still without healthcare, and the country is low on human development indexes. MAF is helping to bridge the gap by providing emergency medical assistance, transporting doctors, nurses, midwives and other healthcare professionals to rural, isolated parts of the country.

Large areas of Angola are still affected by thousands of landmines and pieces of unexploded ordinance. In partnership with the HALO trust and other demining organizations, MAF provides essential transport logistics and local level support as the de-mining effort continues.

More recently, MAF has invested in airstrip development in strategic rural locations across Angola, helping our partners reach communities that had no previous access to vital facilities and medicine. By working closely with national church partners, MAF is enabling them to minister and assist other, more affected communities that are struggling with lack of health, education, and basic economic resources.

As the country makes a slow recovery after decades of war, MAF is facilitating projects, to enable former enemies to come together and work towards a peaceful co-existence and long-term stability. ✚

Main:
Tchincombe
Farm, Angola

Opposite:
The first trial
landing at the
new airstrip
on Tchincombe
Farm, MAF
Angola, 2010

COUNTRY STATS

POPULATION
32.5 million

CAPITAL
Luanda

LANGUAGES
Portuguese,
Umbundu + various
local dialects

ROADS
16,155 miles, mostly
unpaved (245,000
in the UK)

LIFE EXPECTANCY
61.3 years

CLIMATE
Tropical and rainy,
two dry seasons

MAF AIRSTRIPS
28

MAF PARTNERS
31 organisations

FLEET
1 x Cessna 208
2 x Cessna 182 SMA

Luanda

ANGOLA

D.R.C.

NAMIBIA

> "If it weren't for MAF, we wouldn't have come here. MAF has become critical in multiplying what little resources we have."
>
> **Dr Stephen Foster**
> Medical Director for *Centro Evangélico de Medicina do Lubango* (CEML)

TIMELINE

1975 Independence from Portugal, civil war begins

1987 The Church in Angola requests an MAF service

1989 MAF programme launched in Angola

1992 King Air 200 aircraft added to fleet

1993 Failed democratic elections restarted civil war, MAF families evacuated to Namibia

1994 Peace agreement allows MAF families to return and a second base opens in Luanda

1997 Princess Diana visits Angola to support the HALO Trust by raising global awareness of de-mining

2002 Final end to civil war

2003 MAF's global survey 'Operation Access' provides insights for NGOs working in Angola

2005 MAF begins a flying doctor service

2009 MAF assists with relief efforts following severe flooding in southern Angola

2013 Two Cessna 182 SMA aircraft join the fleet

Angola

AIRSTRIP OPENING:
JOURNEY INTO ANOTHER WORLD

A first-hand account from Sally Levett, MAF News Editor and Public Affairs Manager, 1988.

Here in the elephant-and-lion country of the semi-forested savanna-bush, I received my first impressions of this incredible continent and the warm, friendly Tanzanian people.

Just after my arrival, MAF Pilot John Clifford took me on a two-day safari by four-wheel drive to site an airstrip at a remote village. This journey gave me a glimpse of Africa that I will remember with joy all my life.

The village – Magazini – is on the far side of the river Sasawaa, which means that during the rainy season it is completely cut-off. The road through the bush is only a deeply-rutted track winding its way through ten-foot tall grass and semi-forest. The track is, in many places, invisible to the untrained eye.

The 50-mile journey will take 25 minutes in an aircraft, in the mission vehicle it took over 5 hours at a spine-jarring crawl. I cannot imagine a more vivid illustration of the need for MAF in Africa.

Having sited the strip – which took 3½ hours – we returned after dark to Mjimwena to spend the night. On our return journey, our cargo was boosted by gifts of several chickens and two doves – a sheep was offered but thankfully did not materialise!

Right: MAF Pilot John Clifford and Magazini village elders siting airstrip

Opposite, left to right: On the 'road' to Magazini; A world of beauty

En route we got stuck and had to dig ourselves out. While this was going on, I wondered about the lions that roam thereabouts.

As we sat around the fires in the dark, words from Psalm 33 came to mind: 'By the word of the LORD the heavens were made, their starry host by the breath of his mouth.' (Psalm 33:6). Never had the Lord's presence seemed closer.

For me, this was a journey into another world. A stark, but beautiful world. A world of contrasts and extremes, of drought and rains, of beauty and need, of despair, hope and much laughter. Above all, the people – who lack so many things – are overwhelmingly warm and generous. They have not yet allowed time to dominate them as it does us. People are still a priority. ✛

MAF families evacuated from
Kinshasa, **DRC**; 8 out of 15
aircraft damaged by soldiers

Finland, Denmark and **Norway**
join MAF **Europe**

Survey of **Mongolia**

Programme restarts in **Ethiopia**

MAF **France** and MAF **Germany** formed

CRMF moves to Goroka, **PNG**

MAF provides support after the
Rwandan genocide

MAF establishes an email hub
service to respond to the Ebola
outbreak in the **DRC**

1990   **1991** **1992**   **1993** **1994**   **1995**

6

THE 1990s

The 1990s saw rapid expansion of MAF activity across Europe, Africa and beyond.

Yet while this growth indicated progress and increasing trust in MAF's aviation services, it highlighted the desperate and devastating needs that were surfacing across the developing world.

Where MAF had been forming long-term partnerships with remote missions and local Church movements, suddenly the expertise of MAF pilots and the agility of its fleet were called on to respond in the face of huge national disasters.

The genocide in Rwanda, civil war in the DRC and earthquake in Indonesia presented suffering on a scale far greater than many could have imagined. As MAF joined with key humanitarian organisations including the UN, WHO and Red Cross, it became clear that the MAF was becoming more critical and influential than ever before.

Civil War erupts in the **DRC**, MAF staff evacuated and MAF houses looted

MAF **Italy** formed

MAF responds to the Biak earthquake in **Indonesia**

MAF **Bangladesh** programme launched

MAF operations forced to end in **Ethiopia**

Funds provided for a hangar and Cessna Caravan in **Mongolia**

MAF **Mozambique** programme launched

1996   **1997** **1998** **1999**

ELISHA MOITA

Elisha Moita is an evangelist.

In 1977, Elisha was among the privileged few Maasai who learned to read and write in his village of Pinyin near Lake Natron, northern Tanzania. Growing up rooted in Maasai tradition with no knowledge of Christ, he had an encounter with the Living God, aged 16.

'The Lord called me by a vision, and he told me that I have to change and become a Christian,' he explains. 'I didn't even know what Christianity means, I was Maasai.'

With their own deep-rooted traditions and worship, the Maasai sacrifice to many gods and live nomadic, pastoral lives. Carrying spears to protect their livestock, men follow their animals into the bush to find water, encountering dangerous wildlife and other roaming herdsmen. A Maasai will kill to protect his livestock and his family.

'There are some practices the Maasai can't overcome,' Elisha admits. 'But some, like me, are trying to discover that their traditions are not enough for their life.'

Receiving a New Testament in a language he could read, Elisha began to devour God's Word.

'When I read it,' remembers Elisha, 'my heart became very encouraged.

Since that, I started to speak what is written in the Bible. I did not know anything about Jesus Christ, but I really believe God created me to become an evangelist.'

Obediently, Elisha began sharing his testimony and was sent from Pinyin to Malambo where he started to preach.

'At that time, my life was very, very hard,' says Elisha. 'I used to walk alone

Top: Elisha Moita in Merugoi, Tanzania to visit three separate churches in the area

Above: A young Elisha Moita, a Maasai evangelist, with Peter Empson and the C206

Opposite, top: Evangelist Elisha Moita preaches at a market in Pinyin, Tanzania

Opposite, bottom: Maasai men walk to the airstrip in Olemilei

from one village to another. It was so dangerous because there were many animals.'

Elisha remembers the day he encountered a herd of elephants. 'I was walking from Arash,' he says. 'They chased me, and I just ran. They chased me to the mountains so I could hide. I climbed on a big stone and finally they went away.'

'Then another day,' continues Elisha, "I was walking and met a buffalo which was injured by hunters. It became very furious and started to attack. I had no weapon, so it was a difficult fight. I climbed a tree, and he didn't get me.'

In 1985, Elisha's Maasai pastor, Pastor Lemashon came across MAF Pilot Peter Empson who was exploring how to reach remote Maasai in the Arusha region. After being introduced to Elisha, Peter began to work extensively in and around Malambo, taking Elisha once a month on an MAF plane to share the Gospel.

'Just to fly me from one place to another is very important,' smiles Elisha. 'Now more people can be visited by using MAF. MAF can take me from north Maasai to south – 100 kilometres or more. Not only that, I can fly with other evangelists and we can go as a team, preaching the Gospel and seeing people come to Christ.'

'Before, I was alone with many dangers,' he says. 'Now, MAF is a wonderful help and we see miracles – like flying a sick lady to have her baby in a hospital. I became happy, because evangelism could go further and faster than ever before.'

Elisha has been a frequent flyer with MAF for over 40 years. With his help, new airstrips have been created in forgotten mountains. The *Jesus* film has been shown to hundreds of Maasai and many are turning to Christ. Malambo has become a hub of MAF activity and many new churches have been planted in remote communities thanks to the regular Malambo safari flight.

'We thank MAF so much for having that kind of heart, which is with us in our pain in our remote areas. We are proud of MAF, because it is helping so much.' ✚

DISASTER RESPONSE
RWANDA GENOCIDE

'I sat down watching them,' wrote MAF Pilot Alistair Ripper, 'an endless stream of grandparents, children and even toddlers, trudging wearily by. These people have walked for many days to escape vicious slaughter. They have lost virtually everything.'

Below: Rwandan refugees in Kibumba camp near Goma, Zaire (now DRC)

Opposite, bottom: Benako refugee camp

Alistair had flown into Ngara, the site of a rapidly growing settlement in north-west Tanzania for refugees escaping the horrors of the Rwandan genocide. MAF had been called to evacuate Rwandan missionaries and one small MAF aircraft had made initial flights for UN officials and medical relief workers, who faced the insurmountable task of site-planning a small city which had appeared in three days.

'I was overwhelmed by the scale of the problem,' says another MAF Pilot, John Clifford. 'Toilets, water, shelter, food, care of orphaned children. Transport is a major problem. A truck journey to Ngara takes up to three days when it is wet. Small vehicles must cross a hand-pulled ferry to reach the camp, lorries must make a 124-mile detour.' The need for MAF's services was overwhelmingly clear.

John located a section of tarmac road which could be used as a landing strip 5½ miles south of Ngara camp. Passing details to the United Nations High Commissioner for Refugees (UNHCR), MAF began to help a global disaster response mission that would last many months.

At nearby Benako, MAF UK Chair Viscountess Brentford arrived in a Land Rover to assess how MAF could assist. 'I have never felt so helpless,' she wrote, 'I was overwhelmed by the tragedy and the sheer volume of human misery.'

Authorities tell me the Benako camp will grow to half a million, quite apart from the other camps. Three million are still unaccounted for within Rwanda.

'I found there is not a single senior clergyman in the whole camp,' Lady Brentford continued. 'They had all been singled out and killed.' Canon Onesifor Rwamparaye told her how he, along with 4,000 others, had fled a site that had been bombed. 'Only 300 of them made it. I was speechless,' she said.

From 6 April 1994, after violence erupted following the deathy of President Juvénal Habyarimana when his aircraft was shot down, MAF worked around the clock. Alistair and John's initial flights soon expanded to involve aircraft from 4 bases across 3 countries. Many traumatic months of flying for numerous MAF pilots, hours of logistics by MAF ground staff and countless prayers by thousands of MAF supporters around the world were offered to help the broken nation of Rwanda.

Scenes on the ground were horrifying and reports of malnutrition, poverty and unimaginable trauma flooded international media. The Rwandan genocide became known as the most horrific human massacre since the Holocaust. ✝

> MAF's role is crucial... There is no doubt that MAF and MAP are working together to promote total health to enable individuals, families and communities to work together to transform their conditions."

Rev Felicien Nemeyimana
Medical Assistance Programme
(MAP)

MAF NEWS

Canvas churches have at last arrived for Rwandan refugees to act as a place of worship for those living in the vast refugee camps in Benako. 'It was as though this was the first ray of hope in a shattered world which lay all around them,' said Rev Mr Posein, on behalf of the missions at Benako.

MAF Pilot Bryan Pill has made more than 60 flights to the Ngara and Murgwanza camps, delivering five circus tents gifted by Christians around the world.

'Every time I land, a group of children appears,' reports Bryan. 'They never ask for anything but their clothes are nothing more than rags. They are obviously suffering from malnutrition.' Bryan has been distributing new clothes and entertaining the youngsters with Bible stories; 'they love it when I get out my puppet dog,' he says.

RWANDAN GENOCIDE TIMELINE, 1994

6 April President Juvénal Habyarimana's plane shot down. Hutu extremists immediately begin a ruthless genocide against the minority Tutsi community

13 April MAF flies to Ngara. John Clifford transports CARE workers and Bryan Pill makes two rescue trips for mission partners

20 April A Red Cross worker declares Rwanda is the 'worst human disaster we can recall.'

22 April Death toll in Rwanda reaches 100,000 – 1 in 80 people

30 April Death toll thought to be as many as 500,000. MAF Pilot Anne Ezinga flies Central Church of Tanzania to Ngara camp. From the air all roads to Ngara are clogged with refugees; 'a vast sea of humanity'

1 May Red Cross and UN set up the world's largest refugee camp. Water problems threaten a cholera outbreak

4 May Airstrip widened at Ngara following John Clifford's assessment

5 May John Clifford attends co-ordination meeting with the UN at Ngara

17 May Emergency clinic set up by Tearfund and staff at Murgwanza Hospital, crowds swamp the clinic overnight. One baby dies in her mother's arms

17 June MAF UK Chair Viscountess Brentford visits Mwanza, Murgwanza and Benako refugee camps

COUNTRY PROFILE:
MOZAMBIQUE

Despite its tragic history, the Republic of Mozambique is endowed with rich natural resources and beautiful landscapes. Based largely on agriculture, the economy depends on subsistence farming but is also able to manufacture aluminium, petroleum and, more recently, natural gas.

Many years of brutal civil wars and violent communist rule have left the country in a desperate state and it stays one of the poorest in the world – ranked among the bottom ten on the Human Development Index. To this day, the country is dependent on foreign aid and the rehabilitation work of hundreds of humanitarian missions and NGOs. Over half of the population are still below the poverty line and HIV and AIDS rates are among the highest of any country in the world. Life expectancy is tragically only 55.9 years.

Gaining independence in 1975, after almost five centuries of Portuguese rule, Mozambique plunged into 16 years of devastating civil war. Socialist policies and aggressive economic management led to the rise of the Mozambique National Resistance, *Renamo* – a merciless rebel group supported by the Rhodesian government and the South African apartheid regime.

Hundreds of thousands of civilian lives were lost to the fighting, one third of them thought to be children under five years old. Homes were burned, possessions looted and children recruited as child soldiers.

MAF was invited to help in 1985, conducting an initial survey from neighbouring Tanzania. The needs were overwhelming and MAF aircraft began delivering supplies to the far north of Mozambique from Tanzania, as well as transporting pastors to inaccessible locations to speed the development of a growing local Church.

When flooding devastated the Limpopo River basin in February 2000 following two large cyclones, Eline and Gloria, more than a million people were made homeless. Three MAF aircraft based at Maputo were joined by four additional MAF planes from nearby programmes to deliver lifesaving help to the worst-hit areas. The MAF hangar became a flight command centre, and tonnes of food, tents, blankets and medical supplies were distributed to people stranded in treetops and on floating debris. Camera crews travelled by MAF aircraft to send a message to the world of the intense suffering of an already-devastated nation.

When a peace settlement brought a tenuous end to civil war in 1992, Mozambique saw a period of unprecedented growth of around 8% per year, although poverty was still widespread and resources were far from equally distributed. Hope of ongoing economic prosperity was hampered by a high-profile scandal, revealing deep-set government corruption and a sharp decrease in the value of Mozambique's exports which followed in 2016.

Today, MAF continues to provide vital aviation services to mission agencies, national Churches and NGOs, who are working in the poorest and most isolated communities. With MAF's help, a journey that would require two or three days across dangerous, non-existent roads only takes an hour, or even minutes, by MAF aircraft.

MAF's ongoing vision is to facilitate the spread of the Gospel to communities that are yet to receive the message of Christ. A flying doctor programme launched in 2017 perfectly combines medical help with Christian outreach to transform the lives of those living in physical and spiritual darkness. ✠

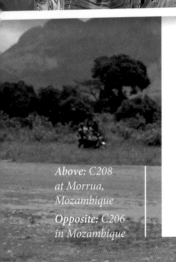

*Above: C208
at Morrua,
Mozambique*

*Opposite: C206
in Mozambique*

COUNTRY STATS

👤 **POPULATION**
29.5 million

☆ **CAPITAL**
Maputo

💬 **LANGUAGES**
Portuguese,
Emakhuwa + local
dialects

🚩 **ROADS**
19,314 miles, mostly
unpaved (245,000
in the UK)

☀ **CLIMATE**
Tropical

〰 **LIFE EXPECTANCY**
55.9 years

🚩 **MAF AIRSTRIPS**
71

🔗 **MAF PARTNERS**
57 organisations

✈ **FLEET**
1 x Cessna 208
1 x Cessna 206

MOZAMBIQUE

☆ Maputo

> Once again, I want to thank you. We were out of supplies and would have had to go a whole day's drive. Through your ministry, we can stick out the rest of the year and see the discipling of Bible teachers, the teaching of new believers and the current literacy classes continue."
>
> **Francois Hattingh**
> Ethnos360

TIMELINE

- **1975** Independence from Portugal
- **1985** MAF begins a survey in Mozambique
- **1988** Pope John Paul II visits Mozambique; the Ministry of Health launches an HIV/AIDS programme
- **1992** Civil war finally comes to an end
- **1994** First multi-party elections held, *Renamo* wins 122 of 250 seats
- **1999** MAF programme launched in Nampula
- **2000** Massive flooding in the south displaces thousands, MAF helps coordinate disaster response
- **2009** MAF helps create MozMed to assist with rural health projects
- **2016** Additional Cessna Grand Caravan joins the fleet, a larger hangar is built
- **2017** MAF launches Flying Doctor programme
- **2019** Cyclones Idai and Kenneth hit Mozambique, MAF is key to response efforts

Mozambique

AIRSTRIP OPENING:
CONQUERING THE MOUNTAINS

An account from MAF News, Rusaru, Uganda. Summer 1995.

Below: Paul Leary with the MAF Cessna 210 at Bundibugyo

Inset: Front cover May – July 1994 MAF News featured Paul Leary and John Skidmore negotiating suitable land for airstrip

Opposite: General flight view of Ugandan village

The clear skies and breathtaking views of snow-capped mountains made it a picture-postcard setting, but it also meant that this remote village was incredibly difficult to reach.

As Herman van Heuvelen eased his single-engined aircraft into its final turn towards the long green airstrip, the anticipation of this moment was profound. Crowds lined the grassway and he could sense a gasp of joy as the wheels hit the soft ground. Paul Leary, a local missionary, waved with glee. This was the culmination of his impossible vision and the result of many months of hard work.

Paul and his wife Lynn had lived with their two children in the Ugandan village of Rusaru, Bundibugyo, for two years. The mountains cut them off from the rest of the country and unpredictable weather left them isolated for much of the year. Despite the near impossibility, Paul decided to build an airstrip.

When Paul appealed to MAF, an initial survey could find no flat area for miles amid the dense jungle, but finally, one flat, open space was discovered. Over many months, Paul, his team and the local Baamba people cleared and levelled a place to land.

Now, as Herman cut the engine, people began running towards the machine, wanting to touch the vessel that had appeared from the sky.

The shadow of witchcraft ran deep in these jungles, but soon the light of the Gospel could be spread far and wide.

MAF News

Special feature: A NEW KIND OF DAWN

Perhaps for the 100,000 Baamba people living in this far-flung jungle of western Uganda, they would no longer need to forage for three months to collect enough berries to stay alive. Perhaps the two mission doctors could receive enough supplies to keep a clinic running. Perhaps more than half the children would survive past their fifth birthday. Perhaps the Bible translators currently devising a written language for the community would see a printed book in Baamban hands.

Within a few weeks the usefulness of the airstrip was made very clear.

When two passengers were injured and the driver killed in a truck crash, Paul was able to visit the injured, who were flown back to their families. 'Being able to fly made the difficult time more bearable,' reflects Paul. 'We were able to be there when support was needed, offer a shoulder to cry on, a place to stay, a friend to listen. With this airstrip we can work so much more effectively.'

For the mission team, great encouragement and comfort has landed in Rusaru. The people of Bundibugyo will learn how aircraft can deliver hope of a different, everlasting kind. ✈

WINNING HEARTS AND TRUST

Helping Refugees in Uganda (extract from *MAF News*, Winter 1996).

If there is one business which booms in Uganda, it is the construction of coffins.

MAF was their only way of receiving supplies and all the earthly possessions they couldn't drag through the jungle.

The government estimates that one million people – 6% of the population – will have died of AIDS by 1998. Nearly one in five women who make it to an antenatal clinic are found to be HIV positive. There is one doctor for every 25,000 people.

And the north-west of Uganda is struggling the most, with pressures intensified by refugees from Sudan who have staggered across the border in their thousands searching for a better life.

Camps at Achol-Pii, Adjumani and Koboko are full of refugees reliant on agencies to help them – and these agencies rely on MAF to deliver their life-saving equipment. Airstrips opened at the request of the UN have proved to be a lifeline.

In fact, air is the only safe way in and out of the camps, which sit surrounded by bandits who shoot drivers and burn trucks daring to approach by road.

Hospitals in the region stay open because of access by air. 'MAF is playing an essential role in serving our hospital equipped with 350 beds, which runs the only training school for midwives in the north,' declares Dr Tocalli of Kalongo Hospital, Uganda. 'MAF continues

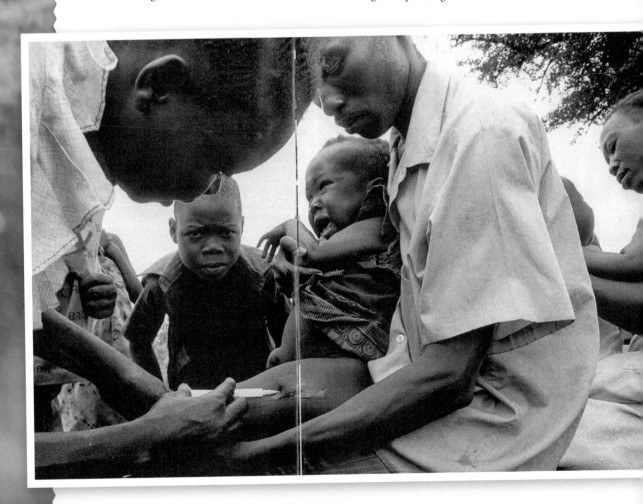

to remain unique,' affirms Dr Onama at Moyo Hospital. 'MAF has won our hearts and trust.'

A new agreement between MAF and aid agencies means flights are provided from Monday to Friday to remote refugee sites in northern Uganda and north-east Zaire, now the DRC. In one of the busiest months, MAF flew ten tonnes of freight including medicines and vaccines requiring perfect transport conditions as well as school materials for refugee children. Aid staff also rely on the safety of MAF to get in and out of the camps.

Emergency flights are also expected, with pilots on standby to help. A four-year-old boy who swallowed a seed which lodged his lung and needed flying to Kampala for urgent treatment. Flown home again by MAF Pilot Bryan Pill a few days later, his safe return caused much rejoicing.

'We thank God for his swift recovery,' reported Heather Komagum at MAF's Kampala office. In an area where action and prayers go hand-in-hand, it's clear that MAF is on the frontline, easing the desperate plight of thousands who are suffering. ✢

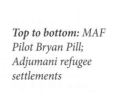

Top to bottom: MAF Pilot Bryan Pill; Adjumani refugee settlements

This page: MAF flew vaccines to remote refugee sites in Northern Uganda

MEDEVAC
JANE'S STORY

Emmanuel hugged his four-year-old daughter Jane, tears streaming down his cheeks. His smile lit up his face as he shared how her life had been saved.

Noticing a swelling above Jane's eye, Emmanuel watched it begin to grow at alarming speed. Living in Kajo-Keji, South Sudan, he took Jane to a local hospital only to be told there was no way they could help. Emmanuel must make a 17-mile journey to Moyo, just over the Ugandan border.

Leaving his wife and two boys behind, Emmanuel began the long walk with his child in his arms. When they finally arrived, the news was devastating. 'We cannot help,' explained a doctor at Moyo. 'Jane has Burkitt Lymphoma. Best to try Arua.'

A further 85-mile journey to Arua, Uganda and Emmanuel was turned away again. Hope was wearing thin. 'Try Kuluva Mission Hospital,' was the advice he received. The final 7-mile stretch in Uganda to Kuluva was Emmanuel's last resort.

Thankfully a miracle was about to unfold.

Encountering various cases of Burkitt Lymphoma in Kampala, Dr Denis Parsons Burkitt travelled to the West Nile area of Uganda to investigate several rural cases, settling in Kuluva to conduct research alongside Dr Morton. Their findings showed the fast-growing malignant cancer of the lymph glands affected many children in tropical areas. Grotesque swellings on the face and abdomen were common and frequently the speed of growth was fatal for those with no access to chemotherapy.

The drugs were expensive – way above the spending power of even the better-off families. Emmanuel had found a cure, but borrowed money was spent feeding his family. There was no hope of raising £200 for Jane's treatment.

Meanwhile, in the department of cancer studies at the University of Birmingham, Professor Alan Rickinson was using ten-year-old tissue for research and was desperate for fresh samples. He would arrange the necessary funding for new tissue to be supplied. Knowing Kuluva had been involved in the research chain, he had alerted Dr Morton.

Desperate to save Jane's life, Dr Morton saw a glimmer of hope. Knowing the sample had to reach Birmingham 48-hours after surgery, he radioed MAF.

Jane's lifesaving operation was timed to coincide with the twice-weekly British Airways flight to the UK. Placed in a special cool box, Jane's tissue was safely stowed on MAF's aircraft and delivered to British Airways. Less than 48 hours after leaving the remote hospital, it arrived in the safe hands of Professor Rickinson. A little girl's life had been saved and hope had been created for many more.

Having spent three, two-month periods nursing his little girl, Emmanuel spoke with deep gratitude to God for the miracle of Jane's recovery and to MAF for making it possible. After more than a year, with no way of knowing if their daughter was alive, Emmanuel began the long journey to reunite Jane with her family. ✛

Below: Jane

Right: A passenger's perspective: flying with MAF to Moyo in Northern Uganda by the border of South Sudan

Opposite, top to bottom: Professor Alan Rickinson; A MAF caravan arrives at Kajo Keji airstrip, South Sudan

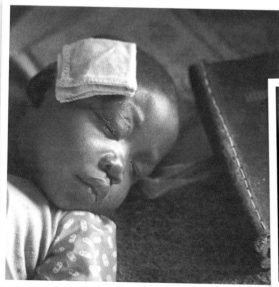

SOUTH SUDAN

Kajo-Keji

>
>
> The daily MAF flight to the hospital in Kuluva was absolutely critical for our work on Burkitt Lymphoma, bringing fresh tumour samples back on ice which arrived in our lab in Birmingham within 48-72 hours.
>
> It was the golden age for our work because we were the only lab in the world generating such newly established cell lines. It was these lines that held the key to studying the Burkitt tumour and its relationship to the Epstein Barr virus. What we learned revolutionised the field.
>
> My team and I are forever in debt to MAF and surgeon David Morton who moved heaven and earth to help us in our research.
>
> **Professor Alan Rickinson**
> August 2020

COUNTRY PROFILE:
BANGLADESH

The partition of India in 1947 saw eastern Bengal become part of the newly formed State of Pakistan. However, political, economic and linguistic discrimination by the Pakistani state led to the Bangladesh Liberation War and the creation of an independent nation in 1971.

Since independence, the People's Republic of Bangladesh has endured widespread poverty, famine and ongoing political turmoil. Violent strikes and acts of terrorism have become commonplace and Islamist violence continues against foreigners and missionaries.

Sitting in the world's largest delta region, Bangladesh is home to almost 5,000 miles of rivers. These abundant waterways are both a blessing and a curse, covering over a third of Bangladesh's surface area. The country's biodiversity includes a vast array of plants and wildlife, including the iconic and endangered national animal, the Bengal tiger.

These vast rivers carry deadly water-borne diseases, which endanger millions of low-income families who dwell along fragile riverbanks and use contaminated water to wash, drink and cook. Annual monsoons cause routine flooding and homelessness for thousands of communities and regular cyclones devastate the livelihoods of millions of people, cutting entire villages off from the rest of the country.

These problems are intensified by climate change; melting glaciers in the Himalayas are raising river levels, increasing tidal heights across Bangladesh, and devastating the livelihoods of 350,000 subsistence farmers.

It was the destruction caused by the Bhola cyclone in November 1970, that mobilised the first MAF activity in Bangladesh. A 20-foot storm surge, which funnelled over the Bay of Bengal, devastated the lowlands, killing at least 500,000 people. MAF's early responders – two men from Sweden – began to envisage how MAF could operate from both land and water to reach millions of isolated people in minutes, rather than days.

Even so, it wasn't until the 1980s that MAF was officially invited by the Bangladesh Flying Academy to assist in the operation of two amphibious aircraft for medevac missions. It soon became clear that a small aircraft charter service could bring help and development to remote communities, enabling thousands of isolated people to access lifesaving help. From then MAF Bangladesh began to take shape.

Registering as an international NGO in 1995, MAF in Bangladesh was finally issued with an Air Transport Operating Licence in 1997 and began operating the only floatplane service in the country.

Today, MAF flies staff of over 50 organisations, which include governments, international NGOs, local charities, and UN agencies, specifically focusing on supporting humanitarian and development initiatives in the most isolated places. Thousands of aid workers, long-term development specialists, surgeons and medical professionals have been able to provide practical help to the most vulnerable thanks to MAF's safe and dependable flight service.

Making a conscious commitment to the long-term development of the country, MAF has employed and trained a large team of national staff, seeing aircraft maintenance engineers, managers, logistics and administrative professionals from the local community flourish with specialist skills.

With invaluable experience of flying across Bangladesh's unique waterways, MAF pilots are on hand to respond in the face of emergency, forming a crucial part of the humanitarian response to frequent and devastating natural disasters. For an MAF pilot, receiving an emergency call for help is not a matter of if, but when. ✠

Main: Southern Bangladesh near the Bay of Bengal

Opposite: MAF float plane lands at Bhola, Bangladesh

COUNTRY STATS

👤 **POPULATION**
162 million

☆ **CAPITAL**
Dhaka

💬 **LANGUAGES**
Bangla

☀ **CLIMATE**
Tropical, with humid rainy monsoon

〰 **LIFE EXPECTANCY**
74.2 years

🚩 **ROADS**
229,351 miles, mostly unpaved (245,000 in the UK)

🚩 **MAF LOCATIONS**
30

🔗 **MAF PARTNERS**
55 organisations

✈ **FLEET**
1 x Amphibious Cessna 208A

BANGLADESH
☆ Dhaka
INDIA

> Without exception, respondents from agencies which use the MAF air service were able to articulate clearly how MAF had enabled agencies to contribute to the alleviation of poverty and the reduction in suffering of individuals and communities in remote areas of Bangladesh."
>
> **Dr David Mundy**
> International Aid Consultant

TIMELINE

1970 Cyclone in Bhola; members from MAF Sweden respond to the disaster

1971 Independence from Pakistan

1980s MAF launches a joint venture with the Bangladesh Flying Academy using a Grumman G-44A Super Widgeon aircraft

1995 MAF registered as international NGO

1997 MAF programme launched

2003 MAF begins a long-term partnership with Friendship's floating hospital, providing safe transport for doctors, supplies and patients

2004 MAF's hangar at the international airport in Dhaka is completed

2007 Cyclone Sidr; MAF responds to the disaster

2008 Department for International Development (DFID) shuttle reaches new remote and vulnerable parts of southern Bangladesh twice a week

2009 MAF responds to Cyclone Aila

2013 Cyclone Mahasen; MAF responds to the disaster

2019 A new Cessna 208 amphibious aircraft arrives

Bangladesh

BUILDING HANGARS

MAF's aircraft maintenance engineers have a vital role in keeping our aircraft well-maintained and safe to fly, but providing them with suitable hangar facilities has often proved challenging.

 **DHAKA AIRPORT**

Below: The MAF hangar at Dhaka Airport, Bangladesh

Opposite: Construction of the MAF hangar, operating under the name Blue Sky Aviation at Buyant-Ukhaa Airport (Ulaanbaatar), Mongolia

BANGLADESH

For example, in Bangladesh, it took 4 years just to obtain permission to build a hangar at the international airport in Dhaka.

The site that was identified was a 5m deep pond near a taxi-runway, so the first task was to prepare the foundations by filling in the pond with sand. As trucks were not allowed into the city during daylight hours, this part of the work could only be carried out at night and it was three months before the team could begin pouring in the concrete foundations.

Meanwhile, a prefabricated steel structure hangar was ordered from Texas, but the shipping containers it was coming in became lost in transit, somewhere in Malaysia.

Thankfully the shipment was found, but the delay meant that constructing the hangar had to wait until after the monsoon season.

Amazingly, the construction was carried out without using a crane: the Bangladeshi contractors erected the steel beams with a steel tripod and chain and the sheeting was put on using bamboo scaffolding. Mercifully, the roof and walls were in place just before the next rainy season.

The final challenge was obtaining permission for the electricity and water supplies, which required 38 different signatories.

Finally, in May 2004, MAF was able to move into the newly constructed hangar, even though water was still being delivered by trucks.

At the inauguration ceremony that month, the Bangladeshi dignitaries that were in attendance heard from several organisations about the importance of MAF's work.

MONGOLIA

The construction of a hangar in Mongolia in 1999, had the added difficulty that the extreme cold required a special kind of resilience from the team.

It had been decided to construct a prefabricated hangar, but after only two days of construction, the Civil Aviation Authority changed the location of the hangar site. New plans were drawn up which required 51 signatories before work could begin.

Thankfully, these were all obtained within a week, which enabled the 3m deep foundations to be dug before the weather became too cold and the ground too hard to continue.

The challenge was then to erect the hangar walls and doors in sub-zero temperatures, so the ground inside could thaw.

When the temperature dropped below -30°C, it took three men to push the hangar doors open.

But when the temperature dropped to -45°C, work had to be temporarily suspended.

Construction of the hangar restarted in February 2000 and continued for the next eight months. Finally, in October, 12 months after the foundations were laid, the last task of laying a special floor covering was completed.

Geoff Hillier, the Chief Aircraft Maintenance Engineer in Mongolia at the time, said of the new facility: 'It is a superb structure, and we are blessed to have the opportunity to set up a high quality maintenance base.'

THE FLEET:
PILATUS PC-12

Arguably the most complex aircraft type ever operated by MAF, the Swiss-built Pilatus PC-12 can fly higher, faster and further than anything else in the current fleet.

With a pressurised cabin allowing operation at altitudes as great as 30,000ft, the turboprop-powered PC-12 boasts performance similar to that of a business jet; all while being certified for operations from short, unprepared airstrips.

MAF's sole PC-12 has served faithfully since 1999, initially joining the Kenya programme as a brand-new aircraft, thanks to the extraordinary generosity of a UK-based couple. The PC-12 was selected in order to bring an extra level of capability to MAF's operations in Africa; the original intention was to provide a high-speed shuttle and medevac service between Nairobi, in Kenya, and Kinshasa, in the

Main: PC-12 in DRC

DRC. However, widespread violence and the eventual breakdown of infrastructure within the DRC meant that this plan had to be shelved. Instead, the PC-12 served some of the most remote destinations in east Africa for the next fourteen years, saving many lives as a highly efficient medevac aircraft.

Over time, this role eventually took its toll on the aircraft and caused serious deterioration to the PT6A-67B turbine engine in particular. A full engine rebuild was required, which was made more complicated and expensive by the PC-12 having an almost-unique variant of the PT6 turbine. An appeal was launched to raise the necessary funds to

put the PC-12 back into service, to which MAF's supporters responded magnificently.

After a few more years of service with its rebuilt engine, the decision was eventually taken to remove the PC-12 from the MAF International fleet in east Africa. The PC-12 was flown to Switzerland in late 2013, to undergo a full overhaul and upgrade programme. After being transferred to MAF USA ownership, the PC-12 returned to Kinshasa in September 2014, to fulfil a role just like the one for which it was originally selected: providing a high-speed service to the remote and isolated people of the DRC. ✛

FACTFILE

GENERAL CHARACTERISTICS

Crew
one or two

Capacity
nine or ten passengers

Length
14.4m (47ft 3in)

Wingspan
16.28m (53ft 5in)

Height
4.26m (14ft)

Wing area
25.81m² (278sq. ft)

Empty weight
2,974kg (6,557lb)

Gross weight
4,500kg (9,921lb)

Powerplant
one Pratt &
Whitney PT6A-67B,
(895kW/1,200hp)

Propeller
Hartzell four-blade
constant-speed,
reversible

PERFORMANCE

Max. speed
272kn (504km/h, 313mph)

Cruise speed
269kn (498km/h, 309mph)

Stall speed
67kn (124km/h, 77mph)

Range
2,000nmi (3,704km, 2,302mi)

Service ceiling
30,000ft

Rate of climb
1,920ft/min

WHAT THE GROUND STAFF SAY

Whether for passengers or cargo, the PC12 is our favorite plane to use here in Kinshasa, West DRC. The only PC12 in our MAF fleet serves missionaries and humanitarian organisations as it can cover the whole country easily in one day — even doing round trips depending on how far we fly. Uniquely designed with an aft cargo door makes loading the aircraft easy for large items like boxes of vaccines, fuel drums or stretchers with patients.

Corrine Cadinouche
Flight Operations Co-ordinator, West DRC

MOTHER TO A NATION

Left: *Glenda Giles with MAF pilots in Papua New Guinea*

Opposite, left: *Dedication of Duna, New Testament*

Opposite, right: *Grade 9 classroom*

Miss Glenda Giles holds an impressive array of achievements, she is a pioneer, missionary and firm friend to MAF.

Born in New Zealand, Glenda began her outreach to the people of PNG in 1967, moving to a remote region with Christian Brethren Churches to work on Bible translation. Completing a New Testament in a local Yuna dialect, Glenda decided to turn her focus to education.

In 1976, she started a High School at Koroba in the mountainous Hela Province, then another in 1987 at Margarima. Becoming a secondary school inspector, Glenda went on to open Green River High School in 1991 and finally Oksapmin High School in 2007, both in the north-western Sandaun Province. The opening of these schools saw Glenda fully dependent on MAF, with aircraft providing the only way in and out.

Now well into her seventies and known affectionately as 'Miss Glenda', she is still teaching at Oksapmin, with a strong passion to educate future generations of local children.

'It brings tears for me,' says Glenda as she reflects on her long-term partnership with MAF. 'I am so grateful to MAF that they bought our papers so these students could sit their exams,' she says, smiling.

Her classroom is light, airy and full of energy. English

posters teach pronouns, verbs and prepositions, illustrated by jolly cartoons in many colours. Sunlight peeps in through tiny cracks in the walls, which are woven from long strands of reed. Its feels like being encased inside a gigantic wicker basket.

On the blackboard is a busy timetable, beginning at 7.45am and displaying a packed week of activity. Each day begins with a prayerful briefing and ends with sport. A poster next to Glenda's desk displays colourful words declaring the name and character of Jesus.

'This is a very remote place, the only way in and out is by plane,' Glenda explains. 'Everything that we can't

produce for ourselves locally is brought in by MAF.'

Outside, during recess, the older pupils are cutting the grass with long machetes. Young men are working on a building project, slicing huge lengths of bamboo ready to construct a big wooden frame for an outbuilding using similar, formidable blades.

'We are very dependent on MAF,' says Glenda. 'They bring in our mail, they deliver food for the students. If we are sick, they take us out. But most of all, they are our friends. They are friends of the students and friends of the teachers. They support us and share in all that we are doing here.'

This friendship is clear to see and the students confirm how reliant they are on MAF's little planes.

Setting a writing assignment entitled 'If Aeroplanes had Never Come', Glenda helps her students anticipate the arrival of their exam papers with contemplation and gratitude.

'If aeroplanes had never come to my valley, my family, my clan and I would be living in the Dark

Ages without a single glimmer of light,' writes Nasep.

'If aeroplanes had never come, most of the people couldn't earn money. MAF brings in cargo, transports sick patients and takes out the vegetables we send to other places. It brings pastors in too!' enthuses Glen.

'Without the plane,' writes Gondo, 'people would have no medical aid, no church and no school. People might not even know who God is. We say thank you to MAF, because the plane came and brought us all of this.'

Like so many schools across PNG, Oksapmin High School is understaffed, crowded and has minimal resources. Yet many of the 120 students will out-perform those in PNG's most prestigious colleges, ranking it among the top ten schools in the country.

These results are a testament to the excellence and commitment of one extraordinary, faith-filled woman and the students she has committed her life to.

'But,' Glenda concludes, 'I can say that if there was no MAF, we wouldn't be here at all. And these children would not be getting the education that they deserve.' ✛

MAF partners with AirServ to respond to cyclones Eline and Gloria in **Mozambique**

MAF's first flight in **Mongolia**

Funds provided for a Cessna Grand Caravan allowing operations to begin in **South Africa**

MAF begins using VSAT communications technology to provide Internet connections in remote and disaster-struck areas

MAF's Nyankunde base, **DRC**, is attacked by rebels. MAF evacuates three plane loads of staff and locations evacuated

MAF-AIR Services, MAF's flight training and engineering base, moves to Mareeba, **Australia**

MAF among first responders to the Boxing Day Tsunami, **Indonesia**

MAF establishes a flight programme in Aceh, **Indonesia**

2000   **2001**   **2002**   **2004**   **2005**

7

THE 2000s

By the turn of the century, MAF was becoming an internationally-recognised and trusted partner.

Responding to more than 20 crisis situations between 2000 and 2009, MAF's skilled personnel formed a central part of global efforts to alleviate suffering.

Demand for expertise became so great that MAF launched a dedicated Disaster Response team in 2006.

Finally, able to return to Sudan, the first MAF pilot family in the country for 25 years arrived in Juba in 2008. While flying increased in Sudan, political tensions were rising in Chad, and MAF was forced to evacuate.

Across the globe, operations expanded in Asia Pacific, with new flying conditions in Mongolia and Timor-Leste increasing MAF's scope and ability to reach the most isolated with the love and healing of Christ.

New base opened in Juba, **Sudan**

MAF **Europe** is reconstituted as MAF **International**, coordinating operations in **Africa and Asia Pacific**

A dedicated Disaster Response department is launched

MAF responds to Cyclone Indiala, **(Madagascar)**, Cyclone Guba **(PNG)**, Cyclone Sidr **(Bangladesh)** and Ebola outbreak in **DRC**

MAF **Timor-Leste** programme begun

Staff evacuated from **Chad** following rebel advancement

MAF launches MozMed, a flying doctor service in **Mozambique**

MAF introduces the new Kodiak 100 aircraft to its fleet

2006   **2007**   **2008**   **2009**

MEDICAL PARTNERSHIPS

 **MAF + MERCY SHIPS**

MADAGASCAR

Like MAF, Mercy Ships use vehicles for the sole purpose of glorifying God and helping the most vulnerable. The Africa Mercy is the largest charity-run hospital ship in the world, boasting five operating rooms, a four-bed recovery area, intensive care facilities and 80 ward beds.

Innovative medical solutions such as collecting and storing blood from its army of volunteer crew members make the Africa Mercy a unique, world-class healthcare solution. With 5 billion people living without access to safe, affordable surgery, Mercy Ships are offering a vital service that has transformed entire communities.

Partnering with MAF while docked in Tamatave on Madagascar's eastern coast, the Africa Mercy helped thousands of patients with treatable conditions who had no access to healthcare. Together, MAF and Mercy Ships offered free, life-saving treatment to the island's remotest people who were unable to make the gruelling journey to Tamatave by road.

> " One of our biggest challenges is reaching the remote. Our surgery has the potential to give life-changing treatment, but we cannot do this job alone – we need God, and we need MAF! Working with MAF is the most effective way to transport patients from isolated areas – some of whom have horrendous tumours. Can you imagine travelling for 20 hours in a crowded bus with a severe facial disfigurement? No one should have to go through that."
>
> **Kirstie Randall**
> Africa Mercy Hospital Director, 2014

mercyships.org

PAPUA NEW GUINEA

In 2018, low immunisation rates in PNG led to an outbreak of polio for the first time in a century. According to the World Health Organisation (WHO), fewer than 40% of births were attended by a trained professional, resulting in at least 2,000 women dying in childbirth every year.

MAF flights ensure that medical teams and equipment arrive quickly and safely in remote and vulnerable regions and hundreds of medevac flights every year save lives that would otherwise be lost owing to the sheer distance from a medical outpost.

One hospital in Kompiam supervises nine remote health centres that are only accessible by air or foot. MAF's 20-year partnership with Dr David Mills at the Kompiam Rural Hospital has saved countless lives and provides a meaningful connection to villages hidden in the rugged mountains of central PNG. Not only has MAF flown personnel and vital medical supplies, but it has transported building materials to extend the hospital facilities.

A new partnership was signed between MAF and Kompiam Rural Hospital in 2018, guaranteeing eight flights to each of the nine clinics every year, at highly subsidised rates. This dependable flight schedule allows the hospital to mobilise the most critical patients and plan immunisation camps. The first flight of this new partnership, to the village of Pyarulama, enabled one of Dr Mills' teams to see 116 patients, including 6 antenatal mothers, 63 children and to administer 181 vaccinations. The walking distance from Kompiam to Pyarulama would have been two full days, but is just ten minutes in MAF's Cessna Caravan aircraft.

Main left:
Mercy Ships in Madagascar, 2014

Main right:
Kompiam Rural Hospital in PNG

"In PNG, we're still putting the foundations down, we're not even close to standing the frames up and putting the roof on in terms of a health service. There's no road network beyond Kompiam, so you either walk or fly. To get a patient out, they have to construct some sort of stretcher and be carried for up to three days. Or, they get to an airstrip then radio to MAF. Without MAF there is no way for those patients to get help. It's critical."

Dr David Mills
Kompiam Hospital

"If this hospital didn't exist, many of us would get wounded in tribal fights, or get sick and die. I got seriously shot by a gun but the hospital was there with its staff and they checked me day and night, so I am alive. I would have died and they would have already buried me, if MAF didn't fly me. We are very thankful for the hospital and health service of Kompiam."

Medevac patient
Kompiam Rural Hospital, 2016

BANGLADESH

Despite healthcare being available at government facilities for a small fee, there are very few medical services in the remoter regions of Bangladesh and clinics have limited opening hours, insufficient medicine and very few trained doctors to meet the needs. In rural areas, there is just one midwife per 100,000 people and sadly 1-in-30 babies die during their first year of life.

As well as offering medevac flights to speed critical patients to hospital, MAF has built meaningful partnerships with numerous NGOs to provide medicine in isolated places. One of them is Friendship, which works with vulnerable people who have limited access to healthcare.

Its three hospital ships bring critical help to marginalised and otherwise inaccessible areas of Bangladesh by travelling along its many waterways. Flying volunteer doctors and vital supplies to Friendship's floating hospitals for over 20 years, MAF has saved hours of dangerous overland travel, allowing more surgeries to take place, medicines to arrive safely and, ultimately, hundreds of lives to be saved.

> "Friendship's mandate is to go to areas which are not accessible, which are the most difficult, geographically challenged areas in Bangladesh. This is where MAF comes in. If we save one hour, it is one person's life saved. So this is a very deep relationship, and it has grown incredibly over the years."
>
> **Runa Khan**
> Executive Director, Friendship

> "I would not have considered leading my team to Friendship's floating hospital had it not been for MAF. I have heard how long, arduous and dangerous overland and water journeys are – we would have lost a minimum of two days and treated many fewer patients."
>
> **Dr Toni Zhong**
> Volunteer team leader
> Friendship Hospital

Ambulance

MONGOLIA

The sheer size of Mongolia, the lack of roads and scarcity of good medical facilities mean that travel to access good healthcare can take days rather than hours. With MAF's initial request coming from Mongolia's Ministry of Health, addressing the country's medical services has always been a priority.

Since flights began in 2001, MAF – under the name BSA – has partnered with numerous organisations working to improve the country's health; often becoming an air ambulance for the sick and injured living and working in very remote locations.

Reaching the Light (RTL) offers therapy services for developmentally disabled Mongolian children living in rural areas – support that did not exist before the charity was founded in 2007. MAF provided essential flights for RTL therapists and patients for over a decade – a partnership that saw transformation for entire families.

Oyantoya, a young girl with cerebral palsy, had lived her entire life with a completely distorted spine, angled wrists and bent legs, not even able to sit on a chair. Her family had never received treatment until MAF was able to fly Oyantoya on a stretcher, along with her mother, to the capital to see the RTL team. The journey would have been almost impossible and would have taken more than 50 hours by bus.

Main left:
Friendship Hospital, Bangladesh, 2017

Main right:
Flight for Reaching the Light, Mongolia, 2017

" I love my daughter so much. I didn't believe she could get better, but now maybe there is some hope. I want her to eat by herself and sit down. That is my hope."

Oyantoya's mother
MAF passenger, 2013

COUNTRY PROFILE:
MONGOLIA

The modern country of Mongolia represents only part of the Mongols' historical homeland; in fact, today more ethnic Mongolians live in China than in Mongolia. Fewer than 3.2 million inhabit Mongolia itself, sprawled across its vast, desolate landscape and making it the most sparsely-populated sovereign state on earth.

Not only is the country enormous in size, but it has vast climatic extremes. With temperatures ranging from 40°C in summertime to -40°C in winter, it is the most varied of the climates MAF's programmes cover and it also has the longest flight legs of any MAF operation in the world. Much of Mongolia is covered by grassy steppe, with mountains in the north and endless desert in the south, leaving very little arable land. Although landlocked, Mongolia has been described as an island, surrounded by a vast swathe of emptiness and endless blue skies.

Soviet withdrawal in the 1990s triggered economic collapse, causing widespread poverty and unemployment. Basic infrastructure and medical services fell into disrepair, with limited or zero access to healthcare among the most remote, rural communities.

With almost half of the population living in Ulaanbaatar – the world's most polluted capital city, fuelled by coal-burning stoves – 30% of Mongolians are nomadic or semi-nomadic, relying on their horses to survive in extremely remote, inhospitable conditions.

The more-recent impacts of climate change have led to severe winters, which often follow a hot, dry summer. With temperatures recorded as low as -60°C, millions of livestock have died and thousands of nomadic families have been forced into cities to survive.

During the 1990s, many agencies arrived to carry out development work, but instantly found that transport to the more remote regions was almost impossible. In August 1990, MAF was invited to help access these areas, by a missionary who had been commissioned by the Ministry of Health to upgrade Mongolia's medical services, following the withdrawal of Russian support.

Initial surveys in the early 1990s saw the arrival of MAF's first family in Ulaanbaatar to negotiate an operating permit. After two long years and no permit, the family were finally forced to leave.

Responding again to further requests by humanitarian agencies and a fast-growing Christian community, MAF carried out a further survey in 1997 and eventually began operating as a joint venture with local partners under the name Blue Sky Aviation.

BSA was the first light aircraft operator to enter the country and has played a significant part in developing general aviation in Mongolia. Research revealed two areas of real need: north of Choibalsan and south of Altai, where people lived incredible distances from infrastructure and where churches had not been established. Thanks to BSA, impossible, week-long journeys were made in a matter of hours.

Supporting vital medical work and frequently working as an air ambulance, BSA has enabled vital healthcare to reach very remote regions across Mongolia, saving many lives and ensuring that medical support can reach new rural locations.

A rapidly growing Mongolian Church was greatly assisted by BSA, and mission trips from the capital were made possible for the first time. It is thought that from just a hanfdful of Christians in 1990 there are more than 70,000 in Mongolia today.

In 2019, MAF was informed that the Mongolian government were introducing new limitations to commercial passenger aircraft operations. After much discussion and prayer, it was decided that MAF's programme in Mongolia should cease in 2020. ✛

Opposite:
C208B in
Mongolia

COUNTRY STATS

POPULATION
3.6 million

CAPITAL
Ulaanbaatar

CLIMATE
Desert; hot dry summer and extremely cold winters

LANGUAGES
Mongolian, Turkic, Russian

ROADS
70,339 miles, mostly unpaved (245,000 in the UK)

LIFE EXPECTANCY
70.8 years

RUSSIA

Ulaanbaatar ☆
MONGOLIA

CHINA

> As we close our Mongolia programme, we grieve the loss of our ministry there and the implication this has for our Mongolian colleagues. We ask for the Lord's provision on every aspect of the programme closure. The Mongolia Cessna Caravan aircraft will arrive in The Netherlands for some minor modifications and be repainted in the MAF livery in preparation for future service."

Dave Fyock
Chief Executive Officer
MAF International, January 2020

TIMELINE

1990 Independence from Soviet control

1990 MAF invited to help assist a Ministry of Health project

1991 First survey of Mongolia

1993 Second survey of Mongolia

1995 First MAF family arrives in Ulaanbaatar

1997 Third survey of Mongolia

1998 Joint venture set up with local partners

1999 Permits obtained for BSA

2000 The 'Millennium Messenger' aircraft arrives in Ulaanbaatar

2001 Flight operations begin

2011 Research identifies opportunities among remote communities north of Choibalsan and south of Altai

2012 Commercial companies begin to increase demand for BSA services

2017 Infrastructure and transport in Mongolia show signs of slow improvement

2018 Need for avionics upgrade increases, amid growing government restrictions

2019 Mongolian government place further restrictions on BSA services

2020 Mongolia programme closes, aircraft redeployed

Mongolia

'The river is coming, the river is coming!'

These were the terrifying words reaching Supardika on Boxing Day, 2004 as he worked near his home. He grabbed his granddaughter and ran for the trees, but other members of his family, including his wife and grandson, were carried away by the rising waters.

> **We saw horrific things. Whole towns had been swept away and only debris left.**

The Boxing Day Tsunami in Indonesia was the result of an earthquake off the coast of Sumatra's Aceh province, killing over 170,000 people and destroying the homes of 550,000 others.

Relief efforts were hampered, as bridges and roads were destroyed or covered with debris, making ground travel almost impossible.

MAF had been working in Indonesia since the 1950s and was one of the first responders, carrying out survey flights and delivering urgent food and medical supplies.

The devastation was summed up by MAF pilot Marco Koffeman: 'We saw horrific things. Whole towns had been swept away and only debris left'.

Several relief organisations asked MAF to lead the co-ordination of the multi-agency response.

Immediately, two MAF aircraft based in Indonesia, a Cessna Caravan from Papua and a Cessna 206 from Kalimantan, were deployed to Sibolga where 40 tonnes of urgent supplies awaited transport to survivors.

The Caravan made daily flights carrying emergency food and water from Medan on the east coast of North Sumatra to Meulaboh on the west coast of Aceh. From there the smaller Cessna 206 ferried aid to remote villages, often landing on narrow sections of road, cleared by villagers.

These aircraft were soon joined by MAF's amphibious de Havilland Turbo Beaver plane, loaned from Bangladesh, which could land in river inlets and even in the sea, with emergency food boxes for communities totally cut off from help. As the plane landed, locals waded into the water forming a chain

> **In the first seven weeks, MAF distributed supplies to some 60,000 victims, by making 1,114 relay flights and transporting 176 tonnes of food.**

Main: Cessna 206 lands on a narrow road to deliver supplies

Opposite, top to bottom: Mammoth waves caused widespread devastation and destroyed the infrastructure; The amphibious Beaver aircraft lands at a village north of Calang, Aceh province, on a daily relief flight carrying over 100 boxes of emergency food supplies

to pass food boxes to the shore. An MAF GA-8 Airvan from Australia also flew in to join the relief effort.

As so much of the communications infrastructure was also destroyed, MAF established communication centres or 'Internet cafes' in Meulaboh and Banda Aceh so that relief workers could communicate with their main offices.

After this, the focus of work shifted towards rehabilitation and rebuilding. MAF aircraft began carrying building equipment and mosquito nets to communities along the coast. It also flew teams with water pumps into remote villages to pump wells and provide clean water. One of those who benefited was Supardika.

Rehabilitation work included clearing debris, building fish farms, planting rice, constructing homes and schools, digging wells, building boats and helping small businesses get back on their feet.

Throughout this time, MAF consistently provided transportation, communications, and logistical help. ✈

> It's great to see how MAF is contributing to the rebuilding. I have flown dentists, builders and many others... there is still a long way to go but the smiles are back on people's faces!"
>
> **Rune Karlsson**
> Pilot

AIRSTRIP OPENING:
FOR GENERATIONS TO COME

Daboto, Papua, Indonesia.

Daboto is about as remote as it gets, tucked into the hostile terrain of the wild Papuan jungle in Indonesia.

Beginning with providing radio communications for New Tribes Mission (NTM, now Ethnos360) workers intent on translating the Gospel, MAF started forging a connection with the village and made a way to reach the Moi people who lived there.

Using the radio network to send requests for supplies, initial aerial deliveries were made by Helimission, but helicopters proved too expensive to sustain the needs of the remote community, and NTM approached MAF to help build an airstrip.

Below:
Carolyn Crockett and some women from the Daboto village in Papua, Indonesia gather for Bible Study

Opposite:
Cessna 206 PK-MPG at Daboto airstrip

Eventually a site was chosen amidst the formidable terrain, and Helimission carefully dropped off a Bobcat excavator. With the help of the Moi, a short strip was created, in the hope of welcoming a fixed-wing aircraft.

MAF experts had reservations about the extremely fine margins of safety at the site – an additional 150 feet of elevation would add security for plane, passengers and pilot. On top of this, the precious sweet potato harvests grew thin and in the meantime, the semi-nomadic Moi labourers had moved on to find new places to plant. This news was heart-breaking for the missionaries who had invested ten years into the community and seen five people come to

Christ. They were determined not to give up.

Finally, an innovative and inspired agreement was made which proved transformational for the entire community.

In exchange for supplies like rice, sweet potatoes and cooking oil, the Moi agreed to stay and continue working on the airstrip. Finding a new sense of purpose, the food payments and development opportunities attracted workers from a neighbouring village. The airstrip development back underway, trust began to deepen with the mission community and locals started to listen carefully to the Gospel.

Within just a few months, 60 Moi came to Christ. The uphill

'no go around' Daboto airstrip – which is often enveloped in morning fog and buffeted by treacherous winds – became the most challenging landing point in the country, but also one of the most celebrated.

Within a week of completion in 2008, Abohapiya lay dying at Daboto. He was suffering from severe abdominal pain and his Moi carers diagnosed that he had 'bad blood'. Using knives, they cut long gashes into his torso to 'bleed him out'. One of the blades lacerated an artery and Abohapiya began to drift in and out of consciousness.

An urgent call was made to MAF.

Two weeks earlier and Abohapiya would have certainly bled to death. The seven-day journey on foot and by boat to the nearest clinic would have proven fatal, but in just 35 minutes, MAF transported Abohapiya for an urgent transfusion with blood donated by his brother. Later, an NTM worker used this lifesaving medevac as an illustration to explain how Jesus gave His blood so that the whole Moi community could live.

MAF Pilot Steve Richards described this as a watershed moment in the Moi people's understanding of the Gospel. Building the airstrip at Daboto not only united missionaries and local people in a profound and powerful way, but their quality of life would continue to improve for generations to come. ✛

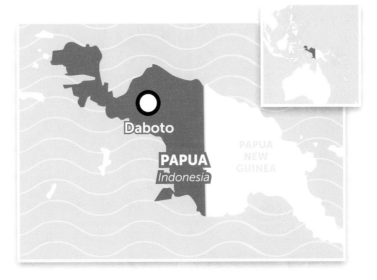

ETHNOS 360

Since the airstrip opened in 2008, MAF has helped Ethnos360 build a clinic and primary school in the village thanks to the access provided by the airstrip.

Today, solar panels help generate electricity and there are Christian nurses and teachers who help the Moi read and write in their own language. Locals have been able to access immunisations from the Papua Department of Health and medical staff are tackling malaria. "Without MAF," says Dr David, "we couldn't operate the clinic at all."

"The health programme here has been wonderful for babies and children," adds Stephen Crockett, an Ethnos360 missionary who has lived in Daboto for 20 years. "There's just a joy that permeates the whole community. God's Word has changed everything for them."

COUNTRY PROFILE:
TIMOR-LESTE

The Democratic Republic of Timor-Leste, also known as East Timor is a country in south-eastern Asia incorporating the eastern half of the island of Timor. Hasty independence from Portugal in 1975 resulted in an immediate invasion by the Indonesian military, who declared the island of Timor to be their 27th province.

Decades of Indonesian occupation were characterised by violent conflict, brutal oppression and the death of at least 200,000 people. When an independence vote was finally recognised by the United Nations in 1999, Indonesian militia ransacked the country before departing, killing livestock, plundering resources and driving a third of the population to seek refuge in the mountains. At the time of eventual independence in 2002, 75% of the country's infrastructure lay in ruin.

In 2003, a survey was conducted to determine how MAF could help rebuild a broken nation and improve access to isolated mountain communities. Forming an official working relationship with the government of Timor-Leste, MAF began working closely with the Ministry of Health to improve the country's dire healthcare needs. Transporting patients, medical staff and development agencies to rural locations, diseases such as bacterial diarrhoea, hepatitis A, typhoid and malaria were found to be affecting vast swathes of the population and could be treated.

Today, over 70% of people still live in rural, mountainside villages isolated from the infrastructure, healthcare and services available in the capital, Dili. Roads are poorly maintained, and flooding and landslides cause frequent disruptions to overland travel. Many communities are still completely cut off from the outside world and rely on MAF, who provides the only permanent fixed-wing aircraft operation in the country.

High levels of unemployment, poverty and lack of opportunity exist almost everywhere outside of Dili, making Timor-Leste one of the hungriest countries in Asia according to the International Food Policy Research Institute. Over 40% of the population survive on less than a dollar per day and most children are vulnerable to diseases stemming from poor sanitation, which keeps them away from school.

Despite the notable revenue generated by seabed oil reserves, infrastructure projects have frequently been poorly-planned and focused on the capital – leaving other regions with no signs of economic progress at all.

Alongside MAF's ongoing work with the Ministry of Health, flights are supporting food production projects to develop markets and help generate income for the poorest communities. By flying in partners to provide access to clean water, hygiene is slowly improving. MAF flights transport building materials, and teachers have seen various schools constructed, allowing young people to access training opportunities in remote areas.

MAF's experience in developing and strengthening the local Church has helped ministry teams to quickly and safely reach isolated communities with the Good News. As rural medical clinics become established, opportunities arise for education and evangelism and MAF has helped connect Christian partners with development initiatives in remote locations.

The services MAF offer are welcomed by the people of Timor-Leste, the government, and development agencies working to improve the long-term prospects of people still struggling to survive across the country. MAF will continue to enable spiritual and physical care to reach people who would otherwise be without help, long into the future. ✙

Right: Sunset at the beach in Dili

COUNTRY STATS

👤 **POPULATION**
1.38 million

⭐ **CAPITAL**
Dili

💬 **LANGUAGES**
Tetun-Prasa, Mambai, Makasai + a variety of local dialects

☀️ **CLIMATE**
Tropical; hot with distinct rainy and dry seasons

〰️ **LIFE EXPECTANCY**
69.3 years

🚩 **ROADS**
3,753 miles, mostly unpaved (245,000 in the UK)

🚩 **MAF AIRSTRIPS**
15

🔗 **MAF PARTNERS**
33 organisations

✈️ **FLEET**
2 x GA-8 Airvans

Dili ⭐
TIMOR-LESTE
INDONESIA

TIMELINE

○	**1975**	Independence from Portugal, Indonesian occupation
○	**1999**	Independence vote recognised by UN
○	**2002**	Timor-Leste declared an independent state
○	**2003**	First MAF survey
○	**2005**	Second MAF survey
○	**2006**	MAF submits proposal for an aircraft to the Ministry of Health and signs a memorandum of understanding to improve healthcare and airlift patients
○	**2007**	Civil Aviation Division of Timor-Leste grants MAF approval; first MAF family arrives
○	**2012**	UN peacekeeping forces withdraw
○	**2013**	Second MAF family arrives
○	**2015**	Second aircraft bought by MAF Australia
○	**2016**	Third full-time pilot arrives
○	**2017**	Peaceful elections do not reveal a clear political leader

> We thank God that MAF was available and we were able to travel to Oecusse to start our ministry... MAF has brought Dili closer to us."
>
> **Myra Leaw**
> Church-planter

Timor-Leste

GIPPSLAND AERONAUTICS GA-8 AIRVAN

The GippsAero GA-8 Airvan is designed and built entirely in Australia, with more than 200 having been produced since its launch in 1995.

Very much a no-frills, utilitarian aircraft, the GA-8 Airvan was conceived to bridge the gap between Cessna's 206 and 208 models.

Although a very useful aircraft in many ways, the one significant drawback of the Airvan is its piston engine, which burns expensive and scarce Avgas fuel; although a turbine-powered variant of the Airvan has been proposed by the manufacturer, this has yet to come to fruition.

MAF operates both the normally-aspirated GA-8 and the turbo-charged GA8-TC320 versions of the Airvan; these aircraft appear identical externally, apart from the three-bladed propeller fitted to the more powerful GA8-TC320.

MAF's Airvans have served in several areas of the Asia-Pacific region, chiefly Arnhem Land in the Northern Territory of Australia and Timor-Leste. They also saw limited service in Papua New Guinea, replacing the Cessna 206 aircraft that had been a mainstay of that programme's activities, but have been subsequently phased-out in favour of larger, Cessna 208 Caravan aircraft. ✠

Main: VH-MFI, Arnhem Land, Australia, 2019

GENERAL CHARACTERISTICS

Crew
one

Capacity
seven passengers

Length
8.95m (29ft 4in)

Wingspan
12.28m (40ft 3in)

Height
3.89m (12ft 9in)

Wing area
19.32m² (208sq. ft)

Empty weight
997kg (2,198lb)

Max. take off weight
1,814kg (3,999lb)

Powerplant
one Textron Lycoming
IO-540-K1A5 air-cooled
flat-six (220kW/300hp)

Propeller
two-bladed Hartzell
F8475R constant-speed

PERFORMANCE

Max. speed
130kn (241km/h, 150mph)
at 5,000ft

Cruise speed
120kn (222km/h, 138mph)
at 10,000ft

Stall speed
52kn (97km, 60mph)
flaps down

Range
730nmi (1,352km, 840mi)

Service ceiling
20,000ft

Rate of climb
788ft/min

WHAT THE PILOT SAYS

The GA8 Airvan is well suited for the type of operations MAF performs in Timor-Leste, namely medical evacuations. The large doorway opening into the main cabin is convenient for loading and unloading stretcher patients with relative ease. The cockpit has a well organised, ergonomic layout and the large pilot and co-pilot side window affords a great view of the constantly changing scenery out of the office window.

Jason Job
Country Director and MAF Pilot, Timor Leste

DR LEE IN MADAGASCAR

Left: *The medical team prepares Liny for surgery*

Opposite: *Medical team members meet outside the school/hospital in Anjabetrongo, a remote village in South Madagascar*

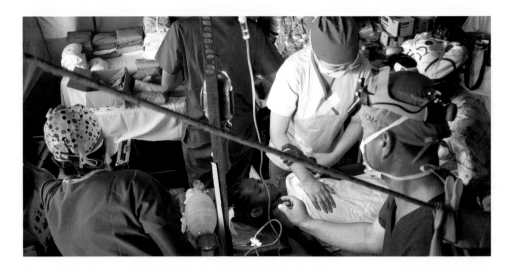

Since the age of 12, Dr Jae Hoon Lee has wanted to be a medical missionary in Africa. Born in South Korea, he trained to become a surgeon, then felt God lead him to Madagascar – a land of incredible need and vast isolation.

'At the very early stages when I settled here, I saw the people in rural areas who have no access to a hospital,' explains Dr Lee. 'At first I wanted to work at a university or government facility. But I thought a mobile medical service was the best way to help. I wanted everybody to receive high-quality medical care even if they live in rural areas. This is my passion.'

Through a relationship with Pastor Jonoro, a missionary living in the far south of Madagascar who had started a school and church, a connection was made with the remote village of Anjabetrongo in the south of Madagascar and Dr Lee.

Once in contact with MAF from 2004, Dr Lee quickly realised that the only way for his vision to become a reality was to fly. 'We cannot access these places by car,' he says. 'To travel to Anjabetrongo would take more than 30 days.'

With the help of MAF, the journey could be made in just two hours.

As MAF's mission to reach the isolated met with Pastor Jonoro's heart for an unreached people, Dr Lee's vision could be put into practice and transformation could begin in Anjabetrongo.

'After MAF arrived at Anjabetrongo, people started to be enlightened,' smiles Dr Lee. Explaining an ancient tradition held by many remote Malagasy communities, he remembers how villagers would take their sick and injured to witchdoctors:

'People were treated with a charm or a medicinal plant,' he says, 'but it didn't work.

'Pastor Jonoro was threatened by witchdoctors because he was the

I had the great opportunity to see what Dr Lee and his medical team are doing on the MMS and spend three days with him. This was his one-hundredth flight in Madagascar! It's amazing to see what his medical team can do under such primitive circumstances. I witnessed an operation on a 12-year-old girl with a tumour the size of a grapefruit. The operating room was a classroom table. They had a mosquito net and a generator running outside which sometimes stopped or ran out of fuel. It was amazing how many people were treated and the complicated surgeries they achieved. For this community it has made a huge difference."

MAF Pilot Kenneth Pedersen
2018

only Christian, passionate to share the Gospel, but he didn't give up. I admired him and wanted to help, the only thing I could do was bring medicine to these people.'

Dr Lee's first flight to Anjabetrongo in 2006 kick-started a regular flight service. Landing to meet a crowd of over 500 patients who gathered at Pastor Jonoro's school, it became clear that the needs were greater than Dr Lee could possibly treat in one day.

So MAF launched the Madagascar Medical Safari service (MMS).

With the ability to stay for a week or more, Dr Lee could carry out multiple surgeries and take a team of nurses and trainee doctors to bring the vision to future generations of medical professionals.

Since 2006, Dr Lee has flown over 100 times with MAF, to the furthest corners of the island. In Anjabetrongo, he has seen a community begin to develop, and a friendship with Pastor Jonoro deepen.

'The first time we arrived here there were only two students at the school. Now there are more than 200,' Dr Lee beams. 'Pastor Jonoro is like my brother now. He is a very brave man.'

Today, people travel as far as 60 miles for consultation or surgery under Dr Lee's team. MAF Madagascar carries out roughly 20, week-long, MMS safari flights every year and thousands of patients are hearing the Good News of Christ.

'Our medical teams have impacted their society,' says Dr Lee, 'witchdoctors have begun to see medical doctors as more powerful. Pastor Jonoro has been protected and they now come to him for help. The Church in Anjabetrongo is standing firm; even though many still cannot read or write, they share the Gospel and even preach themselves. It's so amazing.'

On 9 June 2018, Dr Lee made his centenary landing with MAF, right back where it all began at Anjabetrongo.

'I have found how much MAF contributes to this country,' Dr Lee concludes. 'Without MAF's help, it cannot happen.' ✈

MADAGASCAR MEDICAL SAFARIS

Launching the unique MMS project in 2008, MAF sought to help Dr Lee and other flying doctors who wanted to offer life-changing healthcare in the remotest places. MAF pilots began to transport medical teams to rural locations where bush clinics could run for a week or even longer. An evangelist preached the Gospel, while hundreds of patients waited in line to be seen.

In the last decade alone, more than 30,000 patients have been examined and hundreds of operations performed thanks to MAF's vital MMS service.

IMPROVING SAFETY

MAF aircraft operate in demanding and hostile environments where the rugged terrain brings additional risks to people and our aircraft.

Below: Larry Heintz, MAF International, trains South Sudan team on best Medevac practices for safety and health of a patient

Right: Larry Heintz measuring an airstrip

Opposite: Safety training in Bangladesh with Larry Heintz (MAF and CAA 2013); David Staveley in the cockpit; Marcos Habtetsion, Marco Koffemen, and David Staveley in Nairobi at Check Pilot course

Thankfully, by God's grace, MAF's safety record is excellent and well-respected in the countries in which we work. But MAF has never taken safety for granted and has worked hard to ensure it meets the highest standards and has integrated technological advances, wherever possible, to improve safety.

MAF's reputation for safety and the safety culture within MAF has been greatly enhanced by the work and commitment of two men: David Staveley and Larry Heintz, whose contributions to the field of aviation safety have been recognised by external bodies.

After working for 20 years for MAF, including as a pilot/engineer and then Programme Manager in Ethiopia, David was given responsibility for safety matters in 1989. In addition to implementing new policies and ensuring pilots and aircraft maintenance engineers adhered to stringent standards of safety, David oversaw the introduction of new safety equipment to the MAF Fleet which included bringing the new, 'space age' GPS navigational systems into operation from 1991.

Within just 15 years, these developments meant MAF's rate of accidents per 100,000 hours' flying was reduced by an amazing 80%.

David's achievements in improving aviation standards were recognised by the Guild of Air Pilots and Navigators in 2004, when he was awarded the 'Sword of Honour' by HRH Prince Andrew at Guildhall, in the City of London.

In 1995, David was joined by Larry Heintz, a Canadian pilot/engineer who had served in Chad and later worked as Programme Manager in Ethiopia. David and Larry continued to implement and promote good safety practice within MAF and implemented a Safety Management System which integrated with a Quality Assurance Programme to ensure compliance with new

international aviation standards and legislation.

Larry also set about improving MAF's practice around medevac flights. While at university, Larry had trained as a medical emergency technician and he refreshed these skills with the local ambulance service, who also trained him in use of the Kendrick Extrication Device (KED), designed to keep the spine stable for trauma casualties. He then organised KEDs for MAF programmes and began teaching basic first aid to MAF pilots, showing them how to transport casualties safely.

MAF's excellent safety record and implementation of Safety and Quality Management Systems have led to opportunities to provide advice and training to other humanitarian organisations.

In 2015, Larry was honoured for his work by the UN's World Food Programme (WFP), when he received the Humanitarian Aviation Recognition Award for his outstanding contribution to humanitarian aviation activities.

All Christian service should be the best that we can offer and David and Larry have both clearly demonstrated this by their commitment to ensuring the highest standards possible for MAF Flights. ✈

QUEST KODIAK 100

The Quest Kodiak 100 is designed from the ground-up to be used for mission flying.

The Quest Aircraft Company was set up in 2001 by a group of ex-missionary pilots and engineers, specifically to design and provide aircraft suitable for domestic and international humanitarian applications. The result was the Kodiak, which first flew in 2007.

Now owned by the French aerospace company Daher, Quest have delivered more than 250 Kodiaks, used by missionary organisations like MAF and JAARS (formerly the Jungle Aviation And Radio Service), as well as government-run bodies including the Royal Canadian Mounted Police and the United States Wildlife and Fisheries service.

The Kodiak is a nine-passenger aircraft, similar in appearance and load capacity to the larger Cessna 208. Its great advantage is in being able to land on extremely short airstrips, due to its cleverly-designed wing and powerful engine. The cockpit of the Kodiak is thoroughly 21st Century, with advanced Garmin G1000 avionics helping to both reduce the workload and increase the safety for the crew.

MAF's Kodiaks are mostly operated by programmes led by MAF USA, including one that was donated by supporters from the UK, now registered PK-MEB and based in Kalimantan, which has recently completed 10 years of highly effective service with MAF. ✚

Main: PK-MEF at Pujungan, Kalimantan, Indonesia

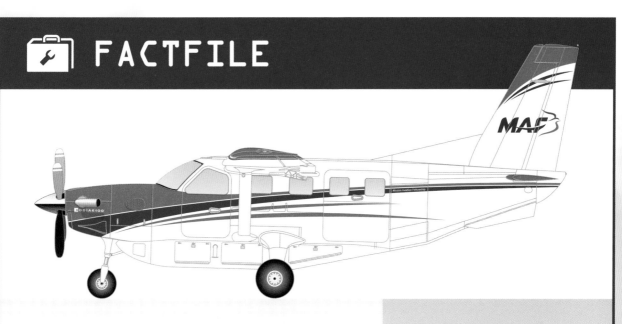

GENERAL CHARACTERISTICS

Crew
one

Capacity
nine passengers

Length
10.2m (33ft 4in)

Wingspan
13.7m (45ft)

Height
4.65m (15ft 3in)

Wing area
22.3m² (240sq. ft)

Empty weight
1,710kg (3,770lb)

Max. take off weight
3,290kg (7,255lb)

Powerplant
one Pratt &
Whitney Canada
PT6A-34 turboprop
(559kW/750hp)

Propeller
constant-speed,
feathering, reversible

PERFORMANCE

Max. speed
183kn (339km/h, 211mph)
true air speed

Cruise speed
174kn (322km/h, 200mph)
at 12,000ft, true air speed

Stall speed
60kn (111km/h, 69mph)
calibrated air speed, flaps down

Range
1,132nmi (2,096km, 1,302mi)
at 12,000ft

Service ceiling
25,000ft

Rate of climb
1,371ft/min

WHAT THE PILOT SAYS

The Kodiak is very well suited for the operational environment in
Kalimantan. The aircraft has really good performance for shorter
airstrips, having been specially designed for short landings. The
Kodiak is comfortable and gets people where they need to go quickly.

David Holsten
CEO of MAF US and Kodiak pilot in Kalimantan

When disasters strike we are so grateful for the numerous relief agencies that are ready with experienced aid workers and life-saving resources such as medical supplies, water and shelter.

But in the chaos and destruction that disasters bring, what they don't have ready is a clear understanding of the specific supplies and people that are needed, where they are needed and the means to get them there.

This is where MAF comes in.

MAF has an operational footprint in 32 countries, partnering with over 2,000 organisations and so is strategically positioned as an effective first responder for disasters and emergencies.

And over many decades, MAF has gained extensive experience in responding to numerous disasters caused by earthquakes, floods, tsunamis, hurricanes, cyclones, rapid famine and food insecurities and medical emergencies like Ebola.

In 2006 MAF established a Global Disaster Response Team under the leadership of veteran MAF Pilot, John Woodberry. The team would be ready at a moment's notice to coordinate a disaster response plan, anywhere in the world.

John maintains a response call list detailing an individual's skill sets, language abilities and other valuable talents that might be needed in a disster. This serves as a pool of MAF aircraft maintenance engineers, pilots, communications specialists, and other volunteers from which he can build an effective response team.

The first stage of MAF's response is usually to conduct aerial surveys where our aircraft fly over an area of disaster, taking photos with embedded GPS information. These photos can be embedded into mapping tools (such as Google Earth or ArcGIS) and provided to the various agencies to assist them in assessing disaster scale and needs so that they can target their resources in the most effective way.

MAF then provides logistics and remote flight support, enabling our partners to respond quickly and appropriately, reaching remote, insecure and inhospitable locations with life-saving help.

There will also be an urgent need for remote communications and so MAF provides Very Small Aperture Terminal (VSAT) communication systems, providing a vital link between field workers and their host organisations.

John summarises this breadth of activity by explaining that MAF is the 'missing piece' that enables its partners to get the right people and the right cargo to the right place at the right time.

But with so many urgent needs and demands, John stresses the importance of prayer:

'The greatest challenge is coming into an unknown situation… so the first thing you do is pray and ask God to give you wisdom'. ✠

Main: MAF Uganda uses 4 Cessna Caravans in the Disaster Response efforts to bring relief to flood victims in Kasese, western Uganda, 2020

Opposite, top to bottom: *Wilbert Rietveld with solar panels in Sulawesi, 2018; Relief efforts in Nepal, 2015*

> " Saving lives, physically and spiritually, is truly God's work. By doing this, we are showing the love of God in action."
>
> **John Woodberry**
> MAF's Global Manager of Disaster Response

INDONESIA, 2018

When an earthquake struck the island of Sulawesi in Indonesia in September 2018, John quickly mobilised a team that knew the culture and language, including logistics staff from MAF's Papua, Indonesia programme.

Two Kodiak 100 aircraft and a helicopter were seconded so people in both towns and rural areas could be reached. MAF also set up a VSAT communication system at Palu Airport which enabled relief workers to communicate with host organisations.

NEPAL, 2015

In April 2015, a massive earthquake, just north-west of Kathmandu in Nepal, flattened towns and villages.

Relief agencies began to arrive in Nepal, but as roads had disappeared, they could not reach remote communities.

Even though MAF did not have a programme in Nepal, it was able to deploy two pilots from the Global Disaster Response Team who secured the use of two helicopters and carried out an initial needs assessment. This identified an urgent need for a co-ordinated light helicopter service to reach more isolated and higher-altitude communities, which MAF provided.

MAF also established logistics support at the airport, helping organisations like the UN's World Food Programme with ramp management, planning, cargo handling and helping smaller NGOs with warehousing logistics and co-ordination.

MAF responds to a magnitude 7.0 earthquake and subsequent cholera outbreak in **Haiti**

CRMF officially becomes part of MAF **Technology Services**

South Sudan becomes an independant nation

MAF introduces a new logo and aircraft livery across its worldwide fleet

MAF responds when Typhoon Haiyan strikes the **Philippines**, resulting in 367 flight hours and 83,000kg of relief cargo

MAF's first survey of **Myanmar**

MAF responds to Ebola outbreak in western **DRC**

MAF **Liberia** programme launched

2010   **2011**   **2012**   **2013**   **2014**

8

———

THE 2010s

As MAF operations expanded, the needs of a fragile and turbulent world became more pronounced than ever.

With natural disasters destroying communities at an extraordinary rate, demand for MAF's Disaster Response Team became even greater .

MAF launched a programme in Liberia to help rebuild a nation devastated by civil war and Ebola.

As it entered its seventh decade, MAF had become a world-leader in the face of humanitarian crises and continued to form a pivotal part of God's rescue plan for humanity.

MAF responds to two deadly earthquakes in **Nepal**

MAF's new training centre is opened in **Mareeba, Australia**

MAF responds to Hurricane Matthew in **Haiti** providing more than 400 flights

MAF responds to Hurricanes Irma and Maria in the **Caribbean**

MAF assists with another Ebola outbreak in the **DRC**

MAF co-ordinates the response to an earthquake in **PNG**

Stuart King, one of MAF's founders, receives the Award of Honour from the Honourable Company of Air Pilots for his outstanding contribution to aviation

2015   **2016**   **2017**   **2018**   **2019**

BREAKING NEW GROUND

Opening a new MAF programme is a lengthy, complex and strategic process, and varies vastly with each programme.

It begins with MAF identifying areas of need where its aircraft and technical credentials can make the greatest impact.

Before a survey, MAF's operations team collects vital information about the country, people, politics and spiritual climate. They pore over maps, books and websites, contacting missions, NGOs and churches already working there to ascertain how MAF's services could improve existing projects and meet the greatest needs.

This essential information is then collated to prepare for several survey trips. These trips assess existing mission activity and identify areas of unmet need in remote locations to evaluate how MAF aircraft could make a

difference. Survey trips are also key for MAF to build strategic relationships with potential partners and form an holistic picture of the local situation.

By the end of the survey phase, MAF must be confident that beginning a programme in a new country will help alleviate suffering and ultimately build God's kingdom.

The subsequent phases can take anything from six months to six years and in some cases, might not result in a new MAF programme at all. From initial research to first MAF flight, there are countless processes, permissions, registrations and contracts to be secured. Each step requires faith, perseverance and a clear call from God. ✈

Main: View of Harper and airstrip in the far southeast of Liberia

Opposite, top to bottom: Max Gove; Liberian flag

LAUNCHING LIBERIA

The initial talks about opening a programme in Liberia began back in 2010 when MAF findings concluded there was a real aviation need within the country. Special Projects Manager, Max Gove, led a series of surveys to the country, beginning in 2011.

During these trips, he identified around 80 NGOs working to alleviate suffering in Liberia. All these organisations indicated they would welcome an MAF flight service to assist their work.

Max also witnessed first-hand the obstacles these organisations faced. With a single day's rainfall recorded at 5m in Monrovia, Liberia's few roads quickly become impassable.

One NGO Operations Manager told Max, 'The biggest challenge we face is getting around in the rainy season. When a car blocks traffic, you're talking about one week stuck on that road. A flight service would be extremely helpful.'

After reviewing Max's evidence with much research, planning and prayer, MAF was delighted to appoint Emil Kündig as Country Director and Chief Pilot, and his wife Margrit as Finance Manager in late 2013. The couple were not only enthusiastic about the new venture in Liberia but had 28-years of MAF experience behind them.

By July 2014, the Emil and Margrit had made preparations to relocate and final operating permissions were complete. Then Ebola hit West Africa. MAF's plans to launch a new programme came to a grinding halt.

It wasn't until 2015, once government offices finally reopened after the Ebola crisis, that national authorities could swiftly grant MAF the necessary permissions to fly. A Cessna Grand Caravan aircraft made its first flight in September that year.

By 2016, MAF had launched a weekly shuttle service to the southeast of the country, turning a two-day journey into a two-hour flight. In 2018, MAF transported more than 20 tonnes of cargo and 3,397 passengers for 136 organisations. With the programme now fully established, MAF's priority is to prepare and reopen as many debilitated airstrips as possible to enable life-saving access to remote communities across the country.

COUNTRY PROFILE:
LIBERIA

Taken from the Latin: *Libertas*, meaning 'freedom', the Republic of Liberia was created in the 1820s by American colonists to provide a haven for freed American slaves. The early settlers developed into a small ruling elite, excluding indigenous tribesmen from citizenship for almost 80 years. The country declared its independence in 1847, but it was not formally recognised until 1862, still making Liberia Africa's oldest modern republic. American influence is reflected in Liberia's flag, politics, religion and culture, with over 80% of people declaring themselves Christians and the Liberian government rooted in the American Constitution.

Receiving some of the highest rainfall anywhere on earth, most of Liberia's landscape is covered by dense, tropical rainforests, which significantly hamper the nation's development and infrastructure. Between May and November, the West African monsoon brings torrential downpours, turning dirt-tracks into impassable quagmires. In the month of July alone, Monrovia, the wettest capital city in the world, receives a metre of rain – almost double the amount which falls in London in an entire year.

A brutal period of civil war between 1989 and 2003 resulted in a quarter of a million deaths. Fuelled by money from blood diamonds, this conflict extended to include the horrific mutilation of innocent civilians as well as the widespread destruction of homes, schools, hospitals, transport facilities and businesses.

A series of MAF surveys identified a real aviation need with an estimated demand for five to six hundred flight hours per year to remote locations. There was clearly an urgency for MAF to begin operations.

Sadly, plans to launch an MAF programme were put on hold following the outbreak of Ebola in March 2014. It saddened the MAF team that our aircraft could not assist in alleviating the impact of the deadly virus which claimed more than 4,800 lives. The social and economic impacts of the outbreak will be felt for years to come, with some 5,900 children losing one or both parents to the disease.

With the country declared Ebola-free in early 2015, MAF staff were able to move into a compound in Monrovia and a Cessna 208B aircraft arrived in August after a five-day ferry flight from Uganda. Since the Minister of Transportation cut the ribbon on 1 October 2015, the programme has seen stady growth and the demand for MAF flights stays very high.

Launching a weekly shuttle service in the southeast in 2016, overland journeys that would take more than two days during the wet season were flown in less than two hours. Demand proved so high that the shuttle has now expanded to three flights each week, delivering medicine, sanitation equipment, education resources and Christian literature to some of the most vulnerable communities.

Today, with 64% of Liberians living below the poverty line and 90% without access to safe drinking water, MAF flights for mission workers and NGOs are a lifeline for thousands of families. Because of MAF, the only humanitarian flight service in the country, ministry and development teams can stay on the frontline for much longer as they can receive frequent and reliable deliveries.

MAF is recognised by the Liberian government, international aid agencies and the church as providing a vital, safe service for their staff. They describe MAF as a lifeline, not a luxury. ✈

Above: Aerial view of the beach at the ELWA compound in Monrovia

Above: Foyo, Liberia

Opposite: Emil Kundig pilots the southern shuttle in Liberia which flies 3 times a week to locations down the coast and in the far southeast of the country

COUNTRY STATS

👤 **POPULATION**
5.07 million

☆ **CAPITAL**
Monrovia

💬 **LANGUAGES**
English + some 20 local dialects

☀ **CLIMATE**
Tropical; hot, humid with frequent heavy showers

∿ **LIFE EXPECTANCY**
64.7 years

🚩 **ROADS**
6,587 miles - mostly unpaved (245,000 in the UK)

🚩 **MAF AIRSTRIPS**
17

🔗 **MAF PARTNERS**
161 organisations

✈ **FLEET**
1 x Cessnsa 208B

GUINEA
SIERRA LEONE
★ Monrovia
LIBERIA
CÔTE D'IVORIE

"
Having MAF moving staff to and from Monrovia, bringing in supplies and urgent patient transfers has been an incredible partnership. I don't know what we'd do if we couldn't call on MAF any time there was a need."

Cate Oswald
Policy and Partnerships Director, Partners in Health

TIMELINE

1862 Liberia recognised as an independent state

1980 Samuel Doe leads a military coup, begins a decade of authoritarian rule

1989 Charles Taylor launches a rebellion which begins 14 years of civil war, resulting in 250,000 deaths, including that of Samuel Doe

1997 Charles Taylor elected to power

2003 Peace agreement ends civil war

2005 Ellen Johnson Sirleaf democratically elected to power – the first female head of state in Africa

2011 MAF carries out two surveys

2012 Third MAF survey

2013 Further visits to Liberia to progress programme plans

2014 Ebola outbreak brings a halt to MAF's plans to launch a flight service

2015 Liberia declared Ebola-free, MAF launches operation with Cessna 208B

2018 The UN completes a 15-year peacekeeping mission in Liberia

2019 Construction begins on new hangar at Spriggs Payne Airport, Monrovia

Liberia

AIRSTRIP OPENING:
A REASON TO CELEBRATE

'The LORD has done it this very day; let us rejoice today and be glad'
(Psalm 118:24 ESV)

Psalm 118:24 had a special meaning for the people of Tapeta, Liberia on 19 March 2016, when MAF Pilot Arjan Paas landed a Cessna 208 on its airstrip that had just reopened after 27 years.

A special dedication ceremony was held to mark the occasion as Tapeta's specialist healthcare services would now be more readily available to those needing them.

The *Jackson F. Doe Memorial Regional Referral Hospital* in Tapeta was opened in 2011 but the poor infrastructure of the surrounding country meant that many people who needed its services had virtually no access to them for much of the year.

Travel within Liberia is complex and difficult: violent thunderstorms are frequent, often leaving vehicles stranded in deep, thick mud for days at a time on the country's unpaved roads.

Roads between Monrovia, the country's capital, and Tapeta are in a very bad condition, especially during the rainy season when flooding often makes the roads completely unusable.

One of the legacies of the 14-year civil war in Liberia was the ruin of a large number of airstrips. When MAF began working in Liberia in 2015, one of its priorities was to repair and reopen as many as possible to give isolated communities a

lifeline to essential services.

As part of this programme, the 800-metre long airstrip in Tapeta was rehabilitated, restoring an essential link with the rest of the country.

The reopening of the airstrip is exciting news, as it represents a milestone for the people of Tapeta and for the patients at the *John F. Kennedy Medical Center* in Monrovia, who need its specialist services.

MAF Liberia's Country Director, Emil Kündig, had the privilege of opening the ceremony in prayer. This was followed by short speeches and remarks from special guests. One of these was the Managing Director of the Liberia Airport

Right: *Tapeta Airstrip Inauguration, March 2016*

Opposite:
Tapeta airstrip, 2016; Difficult travel on Liberia's roads; Emil Kundig, MAF Liberia Programme Manager, at the opening celebration

Authority, Hon Wil Bako Freeman, who noted that the airstrip will ease the difficulties associated with transporting patients, hospital staff, medical equipment and medicine to the hospital.

MAF's arrival in Liberia was the culmination of four years of hard work, involving partner consultations and aerial surveys but was sadly delayed by the Ebola crisis of 2014, when all government business was suspended. This meant that MAF was unable to finalise obtaining the permissions it needed to operate. MAF did not turn away and pressed on in prayer and faith, believing God had called it to serve there.

This determination bore fruit in August 2015 when the first MAF aircraft landed at James Spriggs Payne Airport in Monrovia. MAF's services have since been welcomed by dozens of NGOs and mission groups, who are working to bring hope to Liberia's poorest and most isolated people. ✈

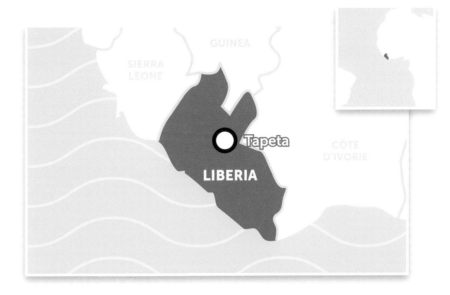

DISASTER RESPONSE
HAITI EARTHQUAKE

On the 12 January 2010 a massive earthquake struck the small Caribbean island nation of Haiti.

Measuring 7.0 on the Richter scale, the effect of the earthquake on the island, already struggling in the wake of tropical storms and hurricanes from the previous year, was devastating.

220,000 people were estimated to have died and over 300,000 were injured. Over 290,000 homes were destroyed or badly damaged leaving 1.5 million people homeless. 4,000 schools were damaged or destroyed.

The Disasters Emergency Committee (DEC) reported that there were 19 million cubic metres of rubble and debris in Port-au-Prince – enough to fill a line of shipping containers stretching end to end from London to Beirut.

How does one begin to respond to such appalling suffering and need?

Ephesians says that in Christ: '...*the whole body, joined and held together by every supporting ligament, grows and builds itself up in love, as each part does its work.*' (Ephesians 4:16)

Such was the response to the Haiti disaster: So many people and organisations responded through prayer, gifts, practical action, delivery of help and encouragement to those involved on the ground. All were important; all contributed to the whole response; all expressed love to the people of Haiti.

MAF's unique part is to provide transport, logistics, co-ordination and communication services for partner organisations. Within 48 hours an MAF team had been assembled in Port-au-Prince headed by MAF's Global Manager of Disaster Response, John Woodberry.

A fully co-ordinated response effort got underway, as MAF partnered with some 60 relief agencies, transported medical personnel and aid workers, delivered critical relief supplies such as food, tarpaulins, blankets, hygiene kits, water treatment systems and medical equipment.

MAF also undertook many emergency medevacs, including a nine-year-old girl called Meka whose feet had been crushed in the earthquake. MAF was on hand to fly her to Pignon to receive care from specialist orthopaedic surgeons.

In the first few critical weeks of the response, MAF had flown 34,620 miles, carrying 104 tonnes of cargo and nearly 1,000 passengers.

Main: The scale of the devastation

Opposite, top: John Woodberry leads the disaster response team

Opposite, top: Unloading emergency supplies

In the face of such devastation, where roads are nearly impassable and bandits threaten travellers, MAF services are invaluable.

Former President Bill Clinton commended MAF for its vital role in the relief and rebuilding efforts saying: 'By organising hundreds of relief flights and delivering thousands of pounds of supplies, you've had a critical impact on Haiti's recovery.'

MAF was also on hand to help combat an outbreak of cholera later in the year by flying medical teams and supplies, including IV solution, to clinics and hospitals. ✈

TECHNOLOGY PARTNERSHIPS

For most of us, the thought of living without electricity, a mobile phone signal or an Internet connection is pretty daunting.

But that is the reality for many remote and isolated communities in PNG.

This lack of everyday things we may take for granted can cause many problems. How can remote villages request supplies from towns? Or arrange for an MAF flight to deliver them? And if there is a medical emergency, how can they call for assistance, or for an MAF medevac flight?

In addition to communication problems, the lack of electricity combined with the difficulty of obtaining fuel for lighting means it is usually not possible to read or study after dark in rural areas.

And for those living in towns and cities, frequent power cuts, sometimes up to ten a day, create significant challenges, especially for schools and hospitals.

Thankfully, MAF's experience of serving remote communities has given it unique insight into these challenges and provided inspiration for technological solutions. ✚

SOLAR POWERED ENERGY FOR HOSPITALS... AND BIBLES!

MAF Technology Services has made solar-powered technology available to hospitals to help them function in power cuts and solar lamps are available to all, at subsidised cost.

This amazing technology has also helped visually-impaired believers to access the Scriptures, as MAF Technology Services have developed solar-powered audio Bibles.

WHEREVER WE GO...

For the women of Nungwaia community, solar powered audio Bibles in their local language have been a huge blessing, with one woman explaining:

'Many do not know how to read, and some have bad eyesight, but the Bible radio is our chance to hear God's Word when we are busy cooking, or when we work in the garden. We can carry it around, wherever we go'.

AUDIO BIBLE IN TOK PISIN

Pastor Kurieva was sadly blinded in an attack 15 years ago when he was shot in the head in a tribal retribution.

But thanks to MAF Technology Services he now has a solar-powered audio Bible in Tok Pisin, as well as in his local village language, which he takes with him wherever he goes.

HF RADIOS IN PNG

Since its earliest days, MAF has invested in cutting edge technology to enable its flights to continue safely.

In order to check weather patterns and the viability of airstrips, as well as arrange flights, effective communication systems with isolated communities were essential.

Therefore in the 1950s MAF began a partnership with CRMF to install a network of High Frequency (HF) radios throughout PNG. Initially these were fuelled by hydro-electric power but are now mostly solar-powered. In 2010, the work of CRMF was brought into a new division within MAF called MAF Technology Services.

This vast HF radio network enables vital communication links with more than 900 locations across PNG and MAF receives over 4,000 calls a year including on average 200 for life-saving medevac flights.

The network was further developed to provide communities with email and Internet access, enabling pastors and teachers to utilise ministry resources and training.

WIFIBibles

The use of mobile phones, especially in urban areas is slowly growing and so MAF Technology Services have introduced another innovation that is proving highly successful: WIFIBibles.

These are small devices that allow anyone with a mobile phone or other wireless device to download Bibles and other Christian resources in nine different languages. These WIFIBibles have now been installed on local buses in Goroka so those travelling around PNG can download the Scriptures in their own language, free of charge.

ACCESS TO GOD'S WORD

Bibles in local languages are hard to obtain in the remote parts of PNG and so the Technology Services team supply MAF pilots with Bible Boxes to carry with them. These contain written Bibles in various languages, audio Bibles, solar lights, reading glasses and Bible commentaries which are then sold at remote airstrips at low prices. Each year, 6,000 written Bibles and nearly 3,000 audio Bibles are distributed this way.

THE FLEET:
DE HAVILLAND CANADA DHC-6 TWIN OTTER

MAF operated several DHC-6 Twin Otter aircraft in Papua New Guinea (PNG) for nearly 40 years, where their rare combination of carrying capacity and short-field performance proved extremely useful.

Coming from a long line of bush aircraft designed in Canada by de Havilland, the Twin Otter was optimised for Short Take-Off and Landing (STOL) performance. The pair of engines from the Pratt & Whitney PT6 family gave the Twin Otters enormous reserves of power, as well as the obvious safety benefits in the event of an engine failure, whilst the aircrafts' wings featured full-span flaps and other aerodynamic devices designed to maximise lift while landing and taking-off. As a result, the Twin Otters were capable of utilising some of the shortest and most challenging airstrips in PNG, despite being larger and heavier than the other aircraft types in the MAF fleet.

The Twin Otters could carry up to 18 passengers, but were most often used to carry heavy and bulky items to remote locations throughout PNG, usually returning full of cash crops grown by remote communities to be sold at market; giving these communities a much-needed source of income.

However, the Twin Otters were increasingly costly and complex to maintain and operate. Pilot availability was a persistent issue, as the aircraft had to be flown with both a Captain and First Officer on board. A decision to withdraw the remaining three aircraft from service was taken in 2018, with all MAF flying in PNG now being undertaken by Cessna 208 Caravans. ✈

Main: P2-MFT at Tekin airstrip, Papua New Guinea, 2016

FACTFILE

GENERAL CHARACTERISTICS

Crew
two

Capacity
eighteen passengers

Length
7.06 m (51ft 9in)

Wingspan
19.8m (65ft)

Height
5.9m (19ft 4in)

Wing area
39m² (420sq. ft)

Empty weight
5,850 lb (2,653 kg)

Max takeoff weight
11,566 lb (5,246 kg)

Power
two Pratt & Whitney
Canada PT6A-
114A turboprop,
(600shp / 450kW)

Propeller
two Hartzell three-
blade constant-speed,
reversible

PERFORMANCE

Max. speed
101 kn (116 mph, 187 km/h)

Cruise speed
158 kn (182 mph, 338 km/h)

Stall speed
56 kn (65 mph, 105 km/h)

Range
540kn (1,000km, 621mi)

Service ceiling
25,000ft (7,620 m)

Rate of climb
1,600ft/min (8.1 m/s)

WHAT THE PILOT SAYS:

'For high-volume passenger and freight
flights in and out of short, steep, rough or
boggy airstrips, the Twin Otter's performance
is in a class of its own and was ideally suited
to the PNG environment and the sort of work
MAF was doing at the time.'

Michael Duncalfe
MAF Pilot and Flight Operations Manager

PASSENGER STORY

MAUD KELLS

'I am with you, that is all you need.' Maud Kells left her home in Cookstown, Northern Ireland in her late twenties with that very promise from God in her heart and went on to serve remote communities in DR Congo from 1968 to 2015.

A missionary nurse with WEC International, who took advantage of MAF flights from the very start of the programme in the 1980s, she is a much-loved member of the MAF family. Out of her many flights there is one that was crucial for her own survival at the age of 75. 'I probably wouldn't have survived if it hadn't been for MAF.'

In January 2015 Maud was living and working in Mulita in Eastern DRC, where she was training staff at a hospital she had helped build and was in now in the middle of building a nursery. Late one night she was tricked into leaving her house by a man hammering on the shutters of her bedroom window and shouting that she was urgently needed in the maternity ward. Thinking it was the patient's husband, she tried to assure him that the midwife and surgeons on duty were dealing with the problem, but he kept insisting that she needed to go herself. Mulita Hospital is in the forest where there are no phone facilities.

After a wasted journey with the night-guard and wondering why she had been called at all, she realised it was a deliberate hoax when they came face to face with armed bandits outside her house. What began as a botched robbery soon turned into a deathly ordeal.

'I was just coming into my compound when, suddenly, two bandits ran from around the back of the house... they were wearing masks and camouflage clothing... I thought it was replica gun that was pointed at me. I went to grab it and immediately of course he pulled the trigger. I was shot through the chest.'

The two bullets entered below her right shoulder and exited her back fracturing two ribs and partially destroying two vertebrae, miraculously they just missed puncturing her lung and severing her spinal-cord! She was in grave danger of death or paralysis.

When after much delay help was summoned, MAF Pilot Jon Cadd at MAF's base in Nyankunde got the urgent medevac call. Shocked when he discovered his passenger was the very familiar Maud, he collected missionary Dr Mathias Holmer and wife Sabine en route, with life-saving blood from Nebobongo mission hospital. He picked up Maud in a critical condition and flew them all back to the mission hospital at Nyankunde, where a team of local doctors continued her treatment.

After recovering in Nyankunda, she spent five days lovingly cared for in the home of Jon and Cher Cadd, then five weeks with Dr Matthias and Sabine at Nebobongo Hospital, who accompanied her on a MAF plane to Uganda, when she returned to Northern Ireland to convalesce.

Devoted to the people she served, Maud said later 'I thought I was dying. I thought, "I'm not ready to go, Lord. I'm still in the middle of building this nursery."

Undeterred, Maud was absolutely determined to go back to Mulita to continue work that she had been doing for nearly 50 years. When she returned in December that same year on yet another MAF flight it was to a warm welcome with much singing and dancing from the entire community. Hundreds of people gathered at the grass airstrip to greet Maud as she arrived – even a brass band!

'All during the years, I could never have continued the work at Mulita,' she said.

'Without MAF, I couldn't have done any of it.'

Pilot Jon Cadd said of Maud 'She is really remarkable. Even though we fly in a lot of her supplies, sometimes she has an urgent need for something at the hospital. So, she rides her bike for a whole day to get to the nearest small town… stays the night and then rides back all the next day.'

And she remains a good friend to MAF. During the 2020 coronavirus pandemic, locked down at home in Northern Ireland and full of her usual fighting spirit, she offered the following encouragement:

'We are living in very uncertain times, but it is so good to know that God, our Heavenly Father is in control... and He has us in the hollow of His hand.' ✝

Opposite, top to bottom: MAF Pilot Jon Cadd with Maud Kells on an earlier evacuation from Mulita; Maud Kells returns to Mulita on an MAF plane flown by David Jacobsson

Top: Maud is flown by Jon Cadd from Mulita to Nyankunde after being shot

Above: Maud is greeted by the whole village on her return to Mulita

PARTNERING IN THE GOSPEL

…and you will be my witnesses in Jerusalem, …and to the ends of the earth. (Acts 1:8)

Over the past two thousand years, the Gospel message has spread to many parts of the world. Revivals such as the Latin American Pentecostal movement in the 1950s, Billy Graham's 'crusades' during the 1960s and the spiritual awakening in South Korea – which saw the Church grow to half a million in the 1980s – are all evidence of Christ-followers fulfilling the Great Commission.

But there are still countless communities, hidden behind mountains, engulfed by dense jungles and, as yet, unreached with the Gospel. It is MAF's mission to see the power of Christ transform their lives.

> **Christ's message of light and hope has proven transformative when shared by Malagasy Christians in a language and culture that rural communities can understand**

In many remote corners of Madagascar, alongside acute physical poverty, lies a tremendous need for the Good News. With 75% of people living on less than £1.50 a day and under the shadow of witchcraft and superstition, Christ's message of light and hope has proven transformative when shared by Malagasy Christians in a language and culture that rural communities can understand.

With the introduction of the economical four-seater Cessna 182 SMA aircraft to its fleet in 2012, a unique opportunity arose for MAF to partner with local pastors so they could access hard-to-reach villages with the Gospel. The project was named MAMAFY.

With a positive response from Christian sponsors around the world, MAF was able to offer MAMAFY flights to local pastors for the same price as a *taxi-brousse* – an unreliable

Opposite and below: A Mamafy flight in March 2019, with pilot Kenneth Pedersen

Right: Children in Madagascar

and often overfull mini-bus that would take hours or even days to travel along dangerous roads. Many of the remote locations were not even on a road map.

MAMAFY, from the Malagasy 'to sow', was officially launched in 2014 and pastors were invited to pay just 10% of the cost of their airfare to take Bibles, musicians and evangelists to isolated communities served by MAF.

Since 2014, MAMAFY has seen the Malagasy Church grow and the message of Christ reach hundreds of new villages across the island. ✚

THE BIBLE IN MALAGASY

"My dream is that every person in Madagascar would have a Bible in their hands," says evangelist Rado Rasoanaivo. Taking Scripture from Antananarivo to Nosy Varika on the west coast would involve two days travel on dangerous roads and one day by boat, but using a MAMAFY flight, Rado and his ministry partner Jean-Claude flew there in little over an hour.

"I have always wanted to go to this town to evangelise, but is has been impossible," Rado smiles. "When we landed, many people came around the plane and we took the opportunity."

Helping unfurl a banner, which unpacked the Gospel message in Malagasy, MAF Pilot Kenneth Pederson watched as Rado and Jean-Claude fervently explain the Good News to the inquisitive crowd. Highly gifted in this kind of outreach, the two preachers handed out a stock of Christian literature and refused to leave until they were certain the locals had understood their message.

"The people seemed very attentive to the message of the Gospel," says Rado. "We pray this Word deposited in their hearts can lead to more conversations."

After finishing the local seminar where they preached and shared a meal with a community 7 kilometres from the airstrip, the pair returned to the MAF aircraft, happy, fulfilled and ready for a second destination, where a similar scenario would unfold.

"In the same day, we reached two towns, preached the Word and left several Bibles," reflects Rado. "After that visit, the Lord allowed a new church to open. May God bless His work and thank you to the entire MAF team and the MAMAFY programme which helps us so much."

HUMANITARIAN PARTNERSHIPS

Bottom: South Sudanese Refugee boy receives treatment for Malaria, by MTI, at Idiwa Health Center III, Moyo District, Northern Uganda

Opposite, top: Beneficiary family of Samaritan's Purse - Fled from Yei to the safety of Bidi Bidi settlement

Opposite, bottom: Tearfund team at the airstrip in Tonj

*F*lying for Life has become a well-known phrase to sum up MAF's mission – encapsulating not only spiritual life, but also the physical transformation that MAF flights can bring.

Hundreds of humanitarian organisations serving those with acute needs have come to rely on MAF. In fact, when people's very existence is on the line, many NGOs know that an MAF aircraft is often the only way to save a human life or bring an end to their suffering because of the precious time saved travelling by air.

Here is a snapshot of some meaningful and life-saving humanitarian partnerships that MAF is grateful to be part of across the world.

CASE STUDY

SOUTH SUDAN

*M*AF has been crucial in the uphill battle to alleviate suffering in the world's youngest nation. Incessant violence and widespread famine have been almost constant challenges faced by its men, women and children who stay locked in vicious cycles of poverty.

Working with humanitarian organisations such as Tearfund, Mercy Corps, World Vision and Medair since the early years of civil war, MAF has ensured that critical food supplies have reached starving mouths in many remote villages and that communities are given the tools to develop self-sufficiently and break the cycle of poverty.

Millions of South Sudanese people have fled to neighbouring countries since violence broke out in 2013. MAF flights continue to support the work of leading organisations, including the UN, UNICEF, WFP, War Child, Christian Relief and Education in South Sudan (CRESS), Samaritan's Purse and the Danish Refugee Council, who all facilitate relief efforts among displaced people.

Bidi Bidi, in northern Uganda, is one of the largest humanitarian settlements in the world, home to some 280,000 South Sudanese refugees. MAF flies more than 450 partner organisations to this vulnerable region, where families are beginning to rebuild their lives in one of the most inspirational and welcoming relief efforts ever seen.

"Samaritan's Purse is providing Water and Sanitation Hygiene (WASH) facilities in Bidi Bidi to combat diseases such as cholera and dysentery, saving thousands of lives.

I got a flight with MAF and the pilot said, "Let's ask God for protection before the flight" – it really blessed and comforted me. It gave me a special reminder that whether you're on the ground or in the air, the Lord is there! If we didn't have MAF, it would reduce the help that would be able to come here."

Charpman Magagula
Regional Manager,
Samaritan's Purse

🔗 TEARFUND

In Aweil, Tearfund is providing practical support to spur long-term development. One Tearfund project aims to boost the nutritional diversity of locally-sourced food and establish financial support for microenterprises.

By involving the local church in these initiatives, Tearfund hopes that ideas of self-sufficiency will take root in the culture so people will be able to remain free from poverty long into the future.

The versatility of MAF's services allow Tearfund to transport different combinations of workers and cargo with each round trip so these projects can become established and grow.

"We are very happy to fly with MAF. In the years to come, we hope that we can continue to make use of MAF's service to reach the remote areas of South Sudan."

Martin Ruppenthal
South Sudan Country Director,
Tearfund

ANGOLA

It is thought that as many as 1.5 million lives were lost and 4 million displaced in the 27 years of fighting in Angola, which finally came to an end in 2002. During this time, an estimated ten million landmines were laid, encircling communities, endangering roads and threatening almost every citizen in the country.

Forming a partnership with the HALO Trust that spans more than 25 years, MAF has enabled its dangerous, yet life-saving de-mining work to reach the furthest corners of the country. Over the years, MAF has provided transport logistics for HALO team members and VIPs conducting site visits, as well as being on call around the clock in the unlikely event of a casualty evacuation.

In more than 17 years, HALO estimates it has safely removed over 100,000 landmines, yet considers their work to be far from finished.

HAZARDOUS AREA LIFE-ORGANISATION (HALO) TRUST

In September 2019, Prince Harry, Duke of Sussex, followed in his mother's footsteps to Angola to visit the work of The HALO Trust.

Dressed in the same type of body armour Princess Diana famously wore in 1997, the Duke of Sussex walked an active minefield and remotely detonated a landmine from a field in Dirico.

On site for the Duke's visit to provide flights for HALO staff, MAF Pilot Marijn Goud had the honour of meeting him. As they spoke, Harry remarked, 'HALO could not do it without you, thanks.'

Main: *VH-MFF in Arnhem Land*

Right: *Prince Harry speaks to MAF Pilot Marijn Goud*

ARNHEM LAND

With unemployment rates among indigenous Australians aged 25-34 years-old around five times higher than their non-indigenous counterparts, many go hungry because they have no means to access food in Australia's vast, isolated homelands. What's more, in Arnhem Land, an average of 60 children a month are removed from parents' care for reasons including neglect and abuse, which ultimately stem from poverty.

MAF flights support initiatives in Yolŋu homelands to produce locally-grown, fresh food and to address the pandemic of curable diseases such as type two diabetes, which persist because indigenous communities have become dependent on longer-lasting processed food. By providing access to essential markets that are simply too far for the Yolŋu to reach along non-existent roads, MAF is providing a way for communities to improve their health and increase their life expectancy.

In flying organisations such as Aboriginal Resource and Development Services (ARDS), Laynhapuy Homelands Aboriginal Corporation (Laynhapuy), Bush Heritage Australia and Yolŋu Business Enterprise (YBE), MAF is helping create career opportunities for the Yolŋu people as well as enabling infrastructure projects, supporting conservation initiatives and preserving and stewarding local heritage sites for the benefit of the wider community.

LAYNHAPUY

Laynhapuy's services include health, accommodation, land and sea management, care for the elderly, homeland services and youth programmes for vulnerable, indigenous communities.

"

Without MAF, I would have had to spend about five hours driving, but the aircraft took 45 minutes each way. This means I can go and work at other communities where my help is needed. My work in these places brings the homelands and communities closer together. It makes the whole of Arnhem Land connected – that is what motivates me!"

Ben Ziegler
Laynhapuy Homelands
Aboriginal Corporation

CONJOINED TWINS

One morning in early September 2017, MAF Pilot Brett Reierson and his wife Jaclyn were humbled to help a remarkable couple and to facilitate a ground-breaking surgery in the DRC.

Below: The conjoined twins before surgery

Right: MAF Pilot Brett Reierson with the twins and their mother on from Vanga hospital to Kinshasa

Opposite:
After successful surgery, MAF flew them back from Kinshasa to Vanga with their parents

As the hot sun rises over MAF's base in Kinshasa, western DRC, pilot's wife Jaclyn Reierson, steps onto a Cessna 206 aircraft for the very first time. Having lived in the DRC with her husband Brett and their three children for over a year, she is thrilled to finally experience first-hand the life-saving work MAF carries out in one of Africa's poorest nations.

But little could have prepared her for the incredible story that was about to unfold:

Landing in Vanga, a 90-minute flight east of Kinshasa, Jaclyn disembarks to witness a large throng of locals, surging around a doctor from the local clinic. Attempting to lead a couple towards the waiting MAF plane, the doctor acts as a shield from the pressing crowd who call, touch and stare at the woman, carrying a small bundle in her arms.

Finally whisked into the plane, Jaclyn helps Brett secure the passengers safely into their seats and takes a closer look at the treasure they are about to fly.

It is a beautiful ball of coloured blankets, tiny fingers and miniature toes - a pair of conjoined twin girls. Delivered naturally deep in the bush, these sleeping babies have survived

an epic 155-mile journey on the back of a motorbike to reach the hospital in Vanga. Their unassisted birth and nine-day life have been nothing short of a miracle.

The twins are joined at the navel, but surgery to separate them is too complex for this small clinic, which is the only medical facility serving the acute needs of thousands of patients in this remote area.

The doctor is clearly amazed at such a rare and astonishing case. 'Born conjoined and naturally, at thirty-seven weeks – it's unheard of!' he exclaims. 'A team of volunteer surgeons in Kinshasa operate on children born with malformations, free of charge. They will assess these babies and can hopefully separate them.'

MAF often transports doctors, patients and supplies to the hospital in Vanga, charging a small missionary rate for each seat. But reserves are set aside for emergency evacuations like this one, which enable patients from the poorest and most remote villages to fly without charge.

'When I was told that MAF could help subsidise this flight, it was great news,' smiles the doctor. 'We began preparations for another long and difficult journey through the jungle, but were concerned for the safety of these fragile newborns.'

With the plane ready for take-off, hundreds of locals line up to wave farewell.

Hazy skies and the drone of the engine create a sense of solitude on the flight back to Kinshasa and Jaclyn enjoys the chance to ponder the events of the day. 'The shared looks between these parents tell me they are enjoying precious, quiet moments to be together as a family before re-entering the world of doctors, hospitals and curious crowds,' she reflects.

Landing in Kinshasa, the family are collected by a medic who takes them for life-saving surgery. All Jaclyn can do is wait, pray and trust that the God who began this astonishing story would bring it to a miraculous conclusion.

Two weeks later, she receives a short text from the doctor in Vanga, 'I just got a call! The twins have been separated. And now, it's time for recovery.' ✈

DEMOCRATIC REPUBLIC OF THE CONGO

GABON

Kinshasa

Vanga

ANGOLA

TANZANIA

Almost one month after this unique medevac flight, MAF flew the family back to Vanga, where they continued their recovery. The separation of twins Anick and Destin was the first of its kind in the DRC, a story that will go down in history.

Pilot Brett Reierson said, *'The natural delivery of conjoined twins is rare enough in a western hospital. But for a mum and her babies to survive this type of birth in such a remote setting followed by a long and difficult journey to be separated – it's unbelievable! It was a privilege to be part of their story.'*

ARCHBISHOP JUSTIN WELBY

Flying the Archbishop to the heart of an Ebola zone.

On 1 August 2018, the DRC declared their tenth outbreak of Ebola in 40 years. Centred in the north-eastern Kivu and Ituri provinces, this eruption of the disease proved to be the country's largest outbreak on record, with the number of confirmed patients breaking well above 3,000 and more cases trickling onto records until early 2020.

Tragically, more than 65% of those who contracted the disease lost their lives.

In late October 2019, the Most Reverend Justin Welby, Archbishop of Canterbury, visited the country to bring hope in the midst of despair – and his chosen and trusted method of transport was MAF.

Reassuring a nervous passenger the night before take-off, Archbishop Justin Welby said, 'You have nothing to worry about, MAF fly in the most difficult places in the world, landing at the most challenging runways and they do it with the highest safety standards.'

Archbishop Justin is an experienced MAF passenger, previously visiting Uganda in

Confidently taking the seat alongside Pilot Nick Frey, Archbishop Justin and his team took in an aerial view of Beni and Butembo, two Ebola-affected 'hot zones' where the virus was being contained by an army of health workers and humanitarian NGOs. On arrival, he was given a vibrant African welcome of pleasure and deep gratitude.

The air heavy with chlorine, Archbishop Justin and his team followed strict WHO anti-contamination procedures as they toured the treatment centres – their shoes hosed by masked healthcare workers and their hands washed every few metres in vats of cleansing liquid. Posing for photographs alongside doctors dressed in white protective smocks, gloves and goggles, Archbishop Justin learnt their names through handwritten badges on foreheads – a method to help very sick patients identify who was caring for them.

Honoured to fly Archbishop Justin and meet those risking their lives to help at the heart of the Ebola crisis, Nick Frey said, 'It's not every day that the Archbishop of Canterbury is your co-pilot! He is a very kind and energetic man of God and it was a real honour to fly him to see the life-saving work taking place at Beni and Butembo. It's wonderful that MAF can play a part by flying key people and equipment to help fight this terrible disease.'

Throughout the Ebola crisis, MAF was on standby to offer emergency evacuation flights, transport blood samples and fly those working to combat the virus. Delivering thousands of vaccines, boxes of scrubs, gloves and oxygen tanks, MAF enabled the WHO to reach very remote areas and became a safe and trusted way to travel at a time of great danger and uncertainty. ✝

Opposite: *Archbishop Justin Welby with Pilot Nick Frey*

Above: *Disinfected wellington boots in the heart of Ebola country*

Below: *The Archbishop is given a vibrant welcome*

Right: *The virus is being contained by an army of health workers and humanitarian NGOs*

2017 and South Sudan in 2014 to honour those whose lives have been devastated by the ongoing civil war.

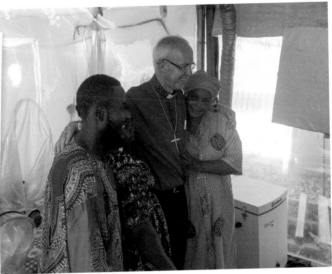

9

INTO THE FUTURE

At the dawn of 2020, we had many plans to mark MAF's 75th year and celebrate God's faithfulness. But none of us knew the unique global situation we would face, and how many changes we would make individually, corporately and as an international community.

Despite the immeasurable challenges and hardships posed by the coronavirus pandemic, MAF has remained strong, prayerful and ready to serve. Holding on to the reassuring words of Psalm 46, the MAF family firmly believes that God is our refuge and strength and He will always help in times of trouble. It is this hope that we continue to fly to the most remote places.

Looking forward, we know MAF's lifesaving work is needed now, more than ever, and we pray that MAF will continue to expand and adapt to meet the needs of a rapidly changing and increasingly vulnerable world.

What a privilege to be a part of it!

Ruth Whitaker
CEO MAF-UK

TRAINING THE NEXT GENERATION

Every day, MAF aircraft fly to some of the most difficult and inhospitable places on the planet.

Main: Flight training in Nampa, USA

Opposite top to bottom: *Keith Ketchum works on the Chad Caravan's bi-annual inspection; John Hermanus, Mareeba engineering support; Glenn Cousley, Mareeba engineering support; Hans Cools and Bridget Ingham in the Redbird Simulator at the MAF Training Centre in Mareeba*

To reach people in isolated communities, MAF pilots need to be able to fly safely over difficult and often featureless terrain, to then land on the most basic of airstrips.

There are no shortcuts for MAF where safety is concerned and in demanding the highest standards from its pilots, MAF invests strategically in training

In March 2015 MAF opened a new Flight Training Centre in Mareeba, Australia, which incorporates a new pilot training partnership with Aviation Australia, to prepare the next generation of aviators to be ready for anything.

This school has a team of flight training instructors with nearly 200 years of commercial aviation experience and over 20,000 hours of flight instructing experience between them.

In addition to a state-of-the-art flight simulator and a flight operations room, Mareeba's airspace, tropical climate, environment, geography and weather conditions are comparable with MAF's Asia-Pacific and Africa programmes.

This ensures the trainee pilots at Mareeba gain the specific knowledge, skills and attitude it takes to be 'mission ready' for remote area operations.

David Graf, an MAF trainee from Switzerland explains: 'This is not a regular flight school, we are learning the MAF way'.

And Danny Gill, an MAF pilot now working in South Sudan, agrees, saying: 'The wisdom and experience the instructors share is invaluable. They are constant reminders of the attitude I need to adopt towards my work'.

MAF does not just require the very best pilots; the complexities of aircraft also demand the very best engineers to maintain and repair them. But there is a world-wide shortage of engineers and fewer engineers means fewer life-saving flights.

Mareeba, which is also MAF's major engineering facility in the Asia-Pacific area, has an apprenticeship programme to ensure there are enough skilled engineers on hangar floors for years to come.

Over the four-year programme, trainees' time is

split between studying at Aviation Australia in Cairns and working in Mareeba.

Keith Ketchum, the Maintenance and Training Coordinator at Mareeba, has worked for MAF for 24 years around the globe and knows from experience that MAF engineers need more than just technical skills:

'Most people think aircraft maintenance is pure science and that engineers are purely technical people, exclusively using logic and reason. But as a Christian I am also responsible for the gifts, time and opportunities God has given me. MAF has allowed me to walk alongside people in every place I have served.'

The Mission Aviation Training Centre (MATC) in The Netherlands also provides high quality and specialised

training and assessment for prospective MAF pilots.

MAF training extends beyond aviation: for example, MAF in Nampa, USA, arranges training for people in technical areas including satellite communications, server maintenance and theological education for national pastors. ✈

Photo: Express Newspaper

COUNTRY PROFILE:
MYANMAR

Also known as Burma, Myanmar hit headlines in recent times following the Rohingya refugee tragedy, which became known as one of the fastest-growing humanitarian crises of our time. Risking death on land or by water, around a million Rohingya Muslims fled persecution, an exodus which was described by the UN as a 'textbook example of ethnic cleansing.'

By January 2020, more than 900,000 Rohingya refugees were living in temporary camps across Bangladesh. Kutupalong in Cox's Bazar has become the largest refugee settlement in the world.

Formally a British colony, Myanmar was granted independence in 1948, but a 1962 coup saw a military dictatorship suppress the country to a closed regime which has endured one of the world's longest-running ongoing civil wars. Clashes between a myriad of ethnic groups seeking autonomy in Myanmar's mountainous border regions have maintained a constant state of unrest, oppression, and poverty.

Like their neighbours in Bangladesh, the people of Myanmar are among the most vulnerable to climate change and extreme weather conditions in the world. In fact, it's thought that 3% of Myanmar's GDP is lost every year owing to natural disasters.

Today 70% of Myanmar's remote communities survive with no access to electricity, and a third of people live under a bamboo roof with mud underfoot and no access to adequate sanitation. Cut off by steep mountain chains and large river systems, many rural communities lack access to the essentials they need to survive.

MAF was first invited to assess the needs in Myanmar in 2013 and began a process of relationship building, surveys and the most complicated airstrip development project in its history.

At the invitation of Dr Sasa, a Christian medic and founder of the NGO Health & Hope, MAF is making his dreams become reality. Growing up in the mountains of Lailenpi with no clinic, hospital, roads or education, Dr Sasa knew nothing would change unless he could help his people. Through a miraculous journey of training and faith via India, Armenia and the UK, Dr Sasa has now trained 834 community health workers to administer medical care across 551 isolated villages. With MAF's help his vision could spread across the entire nation.

Early assessments took up to eight days across the Chin hills – a treacherous journey into the mountains of the remotest and poorest region of Myanmar. MAF teams drove for 10-12 hours each day along winding dirt tracks with sheer mountainous drops. They were among the first foreign travellers to brave these hidden trails, which would likely be washed away during the annual monsoon.

With slopes steeper than 45° and exposure to more than four metres of rainfall, Lailenpi airstrip has proven to be one of MAF's most ambitious and highly technical projects. Hand-drilled cavities four metres deep and larger holes cut by a diesel rig, have extracted soil and rock for civil engineers to calculate the precise slopes and materials required for safety and irrigation.

As MAF launches its newest operation beginning with an innovative mountainside airstrip in Lailenpi, it considers the programme to be a central point of contact for aid agencies to kick-start growth and development across the country. Advocating on behalf of vulnerable communities, one of MAF's key objectives in Myanmar is to help improve rural infrastructure through the reopening of airfields and the construction of new airstrips.

With 75 years of experience, MAF feels there is no organisation better placed to reach the most isolated and vulnerable across Myanmar with aviation and technology. ✚

Main: Rural Myanmar

COUNTRY STATS

👤 POPULATION
56.59 million

☆ CAPITAL
Nay Pyi Taw

💬 LANGUAGES
Burmese

⏱ LIFE EXPECTANCY
69.3 years

☀ CLIMATE
Tropical monsoon; hot, humid, frequent heavy showers

🚩 ROADS
97,500 miles - mostly unpaved (245,000 in the UK)

🚩 MAF AIRSTRIPS
1

MYANMAR

Nay Pyi Taw

MAF IN MYANMAR TIMELINE

2013 An MAF team assesses the needs and opportunities for an air service, which includes a 30-hour road journey hampered by rains and landslides to meet the Chief Minister of Chin State in Hakha

2014 MAF undertakes a comprehensive airstrip assessment of Chin State, making a meaningful connection with the community of Lailenpi. In September, MAF achieves Myanmar company registration

2015 Myanmar holds it first free elections since 1948; Chad Tilley, previously head of MAF Bangladesh, becomes the MAF Country Director for Myanmar, building meaningful relationships with the newly-elected authorities

2016 In partnership with Christian NGO Health & Hope, Heart of God Church, Singapore and Lailenpi community leader Dr Sasa, MAF presents an airstrip construction proposal to the Myanmar government, which is approved

2017 Visitors to the Lailenpi airstrip site include Myanmar's Vice President and Union Ministers; MAF is invited to sit on the Transport and Communications Sector Coordination Group, to influence national decisions on Rural Aviation

2018 A press event attracts 17 media outlets to see the Lailenpi Project, raising awareness of MAF and the project's potential for socio-economic development in Chin State

2019 Construction begins at Lailenpi – MAF's most challenging airstrip development project to date. Thousands gather in Lailenpi to mark the occasion, including members of the Union Government and Chin State officials

2020 With travel restrictions imposed by the COVID-19 pandemic, construction continues at a slower pace in Lailenpi

Myanmar

TO THE END OF THE AGE

Across the world there are still over 730 million people living in extreme poverty. However, due to the 2020 coronavirus pandemic it is thought that, for the first time since 1998, poverty rates will rise as the global economy falls into deep recession.

The ongoing crisis will erase almost all the progress that has been made in the last five years and in 2021, extreme poverty could exceed one billion because of COVID-19.

Studies show there is a direct connection between people living in remote, hard-to-reach places and chronic deprivation, often in very fragile, conflict-affected countries such as those served by MAF. The World Bank has warned that, without intensified action to reach the most vulnerable and isolated communities, the 2030 global poverty goals will not be met.

MAF will be at the heart of this global response and play its part in God's rescue plan for our broken world. There has never

been a greater need for an agile, Christ-centred, humanitarian air-service.

For 75 years, MAF's goal has been to reach places that are inaccessible to the outside world, where communities are struggling to survive without access to basic needs such as healthcare and education – and where their isolation is a barrier to hearing about the transforming love of God.

According to the Joshua Project, today over 40% of the world remains unreached with the Gospel, and our teams remain committed to going above and beyond to make sure those living in extreme isolation are given the best chance to thrive in the fullness of Christ.

In a rapidly-changing world, MAF has

Main: 5H-MSO on the Malambo Safari, Tanzania, 2018

Above and Beyond

become increasingly flexible so it can respond to disasters including earthquakes, famines and conflicts, as well as health emergencies such as Ebola and, most recently, COVID-19. Now seen as a global leader in disaster response, MAF's expert personnel are often at the forefront of distributing healthcare and aid in times of desperate need, as well as rehabilitation in the aftermath of a crisis.

The COVID-19 pandemic has seen MAF prayerfully adapt yet again, to make sure the most vulnerable are protected and that help reaches those in greatest need.

While no one knows exactly what lies ahead, MAF remains true to the vision and passion of its inspirational founders, who sacrificed everything to take the love and healing of Christ to the very ends of the earth. From a handful of weary war veterans, God has crafted a global air-service which covers more destinations than any other commercial airline.

We pray that this life-changing ministry will continue to grow, as MAF forms new strategic partnerships in isolated communities, helps strengthen and nurture the local Church and pioneers new ways to land in the world's forgotten places.

It is our hope that you will join us in the Great Commission, knowing that our Heavenly Father will always be with us, to the very end of the age. ✚

The MAF Prayer

Lord, thank you for your peace,
protection and provision.

We pray that MAF will always have:

One purpose –
the glory of God

One pathway –
the will of God

One passion –
the love of God.

In Jesus' name, Amen.

– Stuart King, MAF co-founder
1922 - 2020

Main: 5R-AAD
in Anjabetrongo,
Madagascar

Acknowledgements

Lead writer and researcher
Jo Lamb

Co-writer and researcher
Pat Finlow

Design and typesetting
Rich Tervet

Content planning
Jenny Davies and Jo Lamb

Commissioning
Vivienne Pattison

Contributors and picture research
Pat Finlow, Stephanie Gidney,
Oliver Nunn (aircraft), Jo Lamb, Rich Tervet

Editorial and production
Viv Wickham

Copy-editing
Beth Dufour

Photo credits

Divyan Ahimaz

Jean Bizimana

John Boogaard

LuAnne Cadd

Sean Cannon

D and S Photography
  Archives / Alamy

Stefan Elser

Express Newspaper

Dave Forney

Stephanie Gidney

Marijn Goud

Mark and Kelly Hewes

Thorkild Jørgensen

Patrick Keller

Stuart King

Margit & Emil Kundig

Dave LePoidevin

Katie Machell

David Marfleet

Matthew Nviiri

Kenneth Pedersen

Jaclyn Reierson

Isaac Rogers

Grant Strugnell

Rich Tervet

Layton Thompson

Katherine Williams

John Wilson

Wise Photographics /
  Clare Wise de Wet

With special thanks to

Becki Dillingham

Corrine Cadinouche

Max Chapman

Andrew Cunningham

Emily Davies

Michael Duncalfe

Nick Frey

Dave Fyock

Dianna Gibney

Stephanie Gidney

Max Gove

Jane Heintz

Geoff Hillier

David Holsten

Tim Houghton

David and Donna Jacobsson

Jason Job

Maud Kells

David Marfleet

Lungpinglak Domtta

Bryan Pill

Anna Rayner

Professor Alan Rickinson

Eleanor Rivers

Kathryn Smith

David and Gwen Staveley

Joy Suarkia

Lindsay Sytsma

Archbishop Justin Welby

Ruth Whitaker

Reverend Paul White

John Woodbury

Notes for further reading

A Bush Pilot's Logbook, Stephen Marshall and Joyce Sklar-Chik, 2019

Flying High, Betty Greene and Dietrich Buss, 2002

Giving Wings to the Gospel, Buss et al., Baker, 1995

Hope Has Wings, Stuart King, MAF UK, 2004

Last Days on the Nile, M Forsberg, 1966

Wings Like Eagles, Clive Langmead, 1991

Country Statistics

Central Intelligence Agency (CIA), *World Factbook*
[https://www.cia.gov/library/publications/the-world-factbook/]